"What an incredible book! Eve[...] choices that can make or br[...] has paved the way for ten concrete and life-giving [...] couple needs to make. Read this book and enjoy deeper fulfillment in your marriage starting today."

Drs. Les and Leslie Parrott, #1 *New York Times* bestselling
authors of *Saving Your Marriage Before It Starts*

"The pages in this book are pages of HOPE! Need a fresh new approach to resolve conflict? Need a new way of creating intimacy? Need to move beyond past hurt? Would you like to have a fresh joy in your relationship? As a mental health professional for over thirty years, I highly recommend Dr. Welch's sound strategies for both relationships in crisis and those that simply desire to be at their very best. This is a resource we use at The Center, A Place of HOPE."

Gregory Jantz, author of thirty books
and founder of The Center, A Place of HOPE

"Happy, healthy, and long-lasting marriages do not happen automatically. They are the result of focused work and adjustments designed to meet changing circumstances. Ron Welch's new book gives couples a fresh approach to address issues that threaten to swamp marriages that otherwise deserve to thrive. Readers will find suggestions, explanations, exercises, and encouragement to face their marital future with hopefulness and success."

James R. Beck, senior professor of counseling,
Denver Seminary

"*10 Choices Successful Couples Make* comes from a man who has 'been-there-done-that' when it comes to pointing the way toward a successful marriage. Ron Welch (a close friend and colleague) has over thirty years of marriage under his belt, more than enough time to define these ten choices and put them into practice in his own private world. Additionally, Ron is a veteran in the graduate school classroom, where he has trained and mentored a large number of men and women who have gone on to be effective professional therapists. Finally, Ron has spent countless hours in conversation with struggling married couples who, under his guidance, have learned to make these choices for themselves. I really like this man, Ron Welch. I trust him, and I consider it an honor to introduce him to you."

**Gordon MacDonald**, speaker, chancellor of Denver Seminary,
and author of *Ordering Your Private World*
and *A Resilient Life*

"Marriages *can* be transformed. Bad habits *can* be broken. Feelings of love *can* return where they have been absent. But none of this happens without intentional choices and hard work on the part of both spouses. Ron Welch provides clear, easy-to-understand guidelines for the *choices* spouses can make to begin the process of strengthening or repairing their marriages. It is *not* a matter of forces outside of anyone's control but what one chooses to do, difficult as those choices may seem. This little book is chock full of hope, wisdom, biblical insight, and proven methods from the counselor's office. Every couple can learn from it, and it ought to be required reading for conversations between every engaged and even pre-engaged couple. An amazing gift to the church and the world from someone who has practiced what he preaches."

**Craig L. Blomberg**, distinguished professor
of New Testament, Denver Seminary

"In *10 Choices Successful Couples Make: The Secret to Love That Lasts a Lifetime*, Dr. Ron Welch has zeroed in on some of the most basic areas in preventing (and healing) fractured couple relationships and heightening couple flourishing. All ten choices are spot-on, but I was particularly impressed by his emphases on forgiving, trusting, being other-oriented, maintaining intimacy, and committing. This book will repay *any* couple's reading in years of stronger relationship satisfaction and enjoyment."

**Everett L. Worthington Jr.** (see www.EvWorthington
-forgiveness.com for hundreds of free resources)

# *10* Choices
# SUCCESSFUL
# COUPLES
# Make

## Also by Dr. Ron Welch

*The Controlling Husband: What Every Woman Needs to Know*

# *10* Choices
# SUCCESSFUL
# COUPLES
# Make

The Secret
to Love That Lasts
a Lifetime

## DR. RON WELCH

Revell

a division of Baker Publishing Group
Grand Rapids, Michigan

© 2019 by Dr. Ronald D. Welch

Published by Revell
a division of Baker Publishing Group
PO Box 6287, Grand Rapids, MI 49516-6287
www.revellbooks.com

Printed in the United States of America

Library of Congress Cataloging-in-Publication Data
Names: Welch, Ron, Dr., author.
Title: 10 choices successful couples make : the secret to love that lasts a lifetime / Dr. Ron Welch.
Other titles: Ten choices successful couples make
Description: Grand Rapids, MI : Revell, [2019] | Includes bibliographical references and index.
Identifiers: LCCN 2018025889 | ISBN 9780800729684 (pbk. : alk. paper)
Subjects: LCSH: Marriage—Psychological aspects. | Couples—Psychology. | Man-woman relationships. | Interpersonal relations. | Marriage—Religious aspects—Christianity.
Classification: LCC HQ734 .W4398 2019 | DDC 306.81—dc23
LC record available at https://lccn.loc.gov/2018025889

19  20  21  22  23  24  25     7  6  5  4  3  2

*To my wife and soul mate, Jan.*
This book is about choices, and without doubt,
you are the best choice I have ever made.
Thank you for believing in us,
for letting the love of Christ shine through you,
for teaching me what love and forgiveness truly mean,
and for walking by my side on this journey called marriage.

# Contents

# Acknowledgments

This book would not have been possible without contributions from the following individuals, to whom I will be eternally grateful:

my wife, Jan, who for more than thirty years has shared this life journey with me as my partner, my soul mate, my best friend, and my one true love;

my two amazing boys, Britton and Brevin, who are growing into men of character and honor whom I am truly proud to call my sons;

my mom and dad, who taught me about hard work, sacrifice, dedication, and the importance of faith in Christ;

my sister, Cheryl, who continues to help me understand the variety of cultures, people, and experiences in the world that my own biases prevent me from seeing clearly;

my editor, Vicki Crumpton, my agent, Greg Daniel, and Revell, a division of Baker Publishing Group, for their continued support and guidance in my writing career;

Everett Worthington and Bill Fleeman, for their professional contributions to this work;

Denver Seminary, for providing the sabbatical time to write this book;

and my clients from over twenty-five years of practice, who have taught me what resilience, determination, and healing truly look like.

*one*

---

# Marriage Is about Choices

They were like so many couples I see in premarital therapy. For Paul and Grace, the future had never looked brighter. "I fell in love with him the first time I saw those beautiful blue eyes," Grace gushed. "The more I got to know him, the more I knew he was the only man for me." Paul was equally effusive in his praise. "Grace completes me. She is everything I could ever want in a wife and a partner. I've never felt this way about anyone—I have fallen totally and completely in love with her."

Aren't engaged couples wonderful?! They are so certain their relationship is the best thing since sliced bread and so excited about their future together. The excitement of the engagement is followed by the wedding celebration and the blissful honeymoon. They feel they are riding a wave of happiness that will never end.

Not to burst this bubble of happiness, but let's take a closer look at what Paul referred to as falling in love. We use this phrase a lot. We have a Valentine's Day image of Cupid shooting an arrow that hits us with such force that we have no choice but to fall in love. Think about it, though. Do we really "fall" in love?

I don't think so. In fact, I don't think it is a passive act at all. Love doesn't just happen to us. I would argue that love is a clear, intentional choice that we make. I believe it is more accurate to say, "I choose to love you."

## "Jumping" into Love

Maybe we don't have much control over that initial desire or interest that attracts us to another person. I know when I first saw the woman who would become my wife walk out in that black dress, I sure didn't feel like I had any control over what was happening to me. However, I wonder if those feelings are actually what love is. I think those feelings might be attraction or infatuation or desire—but not love.

It would be more accurate to say that we "jump" into love. When we literally fall, we view that as an accident; it's certainly not something we intentionally wanted to happen. Love isn't an accident, nor is it a stroke of luck we are fortunate to experience. Rather, I believe love is more like being high up on the diving board at a swimming pool, looking down at the water far below, and making the choice to jump into the unknown.

Making that type of jump is not easy. You don't know what the end result will be, and that is what makes the decision scary. The great thing about diving, though, is that each time you make that dive and come back up to the surface, it is easier to do the next time. Choosing to love your partner is a skill you can learn, and the better you get at it, the less scary and out of control it feels.

→ **I Choose to Love You**

This lifelong choice—the "I love you for better or for worse" vow type of thing—is definitely an intentional, repetitive choice. It is not a one-time choice you make when you stand in front of God and your family and friends and say, "I do." This is a decision you make over and over again every day.

Choosing love is not just about the tough choices either, such as how many kids to have or where to live. These decisions get our attention because the consequences seem so big. You can probably point to several choices you have made in your relationship that have had a significant effect on your future.

Choosing love is the day-to-day decisions you make . . . where to go to dinner, whether to wash the dishes or pick up your socks, what television show to watch. This may be where love truly grows—where choosing love actually happens.

Perhaps choosing love is the choice to get up and calm the baby rather than go back to sleep and let your partner do it. Maybe choosing love is the choice to drive ten miles to get the kind of ice cream your spouse loves instead of the cheap kind at the store close to home. Choosing love can be seen in the choice to keep quiet rather than say that one thing you know will cause hurt and pain. In each of these decisions, you say, "I choose to love you."

**Making Decisions**

Much effort has been put into researching how we make decisions. William Glasser created "choice theory." The big idea here is that people are unhappy because they are in bad relationships, and their bad relationships are based on bad choices.

He believes that when people learn to make better choices, their relationships improve and they become happier people.[1] I believe this means that even the most challenging relationship could be improved if the couple made different choices.

William Samuelson and Richard Zeckhauser wrote an article titled "Status Quo Bias in Decision Making." They found that people preferred to maintain the status quo and stayed with their original decision, even if a new alternative appeared better.[2] Even in financial investing, people choose to stick with what they know rather than jump into a clearly better option.[3]

Both of these ideas are solid. These studies help us see that in marriage, partners may really struggle to change the habits they have formed over the years, even when doing so could improve their relationship. The choices we make in our relationships directly affect our emotions, and the assumptions we make about each other cause us to expect our partners to succeed or fail. But there is more to the story. Our choices are also affected by our values, by the way we think and feel, and by the consequences of previous choices. Even more importantly, we have each learned patterns of decision making from the families we grew up in. We will look at these in more detail in chapter 5.

## Three Ways to Make Choices

Over the years, I have seen couples take one of three approaches to making decisions. Some choose to compromise, others choose to trade off getting what they want, and still others simply allow the person most affected to have his or her way.

### Compromise

Joel and LaKisha faced a difficult choice. LaKisha's mother had passed away a few years earlier, and her father's health was now failing. Family had always been important to her, and she wanted her father to come and live with them.

Joel valued family too, but he wasn't sure it would be possible to balance caring for her father and taking care of their own three kids while both of them worked full-time. He felt that a care facility might provide a better option for LaKisha's father, but she was very much against "putting him in a home for old people." Her father was aware that he could not take care of himself as he had in the past, but he wanted to remain as independent as possible.

They struggled with this issue with little progress for several weeks, until Joel suggested a compromise. "I wonder if we could do both?" he asked pensively. LaKisha looked up and patiently waited for him to continue.

"We agree your dad needs someone to help take care of him."

LaKisha nodded her agreement but then said, "You know I believe that is our job, not some worker in a nursing home."

Joel responded, "I get that, but let's think outside the box here. What if we found a care facility where he could live during the week when we are at work but that would also allow him to live at our house on the weekends?"

LaKisha thought for a moment and then said, "I had never thought about something like that. I don't think you can have part-time care, though. I think he has to live there or not live there." Joel suggested they at least call some places and find out. It turned out that some facilities offered full-day programs, but they could not find any that allowed residents to live there only during the week.

After some additional negotiating, they agreed to compromise by having LaKisha's father attend a program during the day, hiring an in-home caregiver for the evenings, and caring for him themselves during the night and on the weekends. They would have to trade off at night sometimes, but they had done that when their children were younger.

In many situations, as this couple discovered, there are options that neither person has thought of. Sometimes people need outside input to come up with these alternatives. Often, compromise can lead to a solution that allows both parties to get at least some of what they want.

### Trade Off

At least once each year, usually in early March, Maria and Lucas had the same discussion. One of them would ask, "Where should we go on vacation this year?" Lucas had a couple of weeks he could take off in June or July, and as a teacher, Maria had summers off. They always had difficulty figuring out where to go, and they would eventually compromise on some place they could both live with but neither really loved.

This particular year Maria wanted to go to a beach in California, but she knew Lucas didn't like sitting on the beach and wanted to go to the mountains. In the past, they would have ended up somewhere like Las Vegas, which neither really wanted. This time Maria said, "I've got an idea, Lucas. What if we go to the beach this year, and you share that with me, and next year we go to the mountains, and I share that with you?"

Lucas thought for a minute. "So this year you get to do what you want, and next year I get to do what I want, and we don't have to settle for something neither of us wants?"

Maria said, "Yes, that's it exactly! What do you think?"

Lucas smiled and said, "This seems pretty simple. Why didn't we think of this sooner?"

In contrast to the first couple, these partners discovered that they didn't want to settle for a compromise. They wanted to find a way they could each have exactly what they wanted (at least some of the time). The trade-off allowed each to sacrifice at one point and then get what they wanted at another time.

### Allow the Person Most Affected to Decide

After ten years of marriage, Lance and Kelly were faced with a big decision that involved Kelly's job. She had the opportunity for a promotion, but it would mean moving the family to Texas. Lance was close to his brothers and parents, who all lived in Colorado, which would make a move difficult for him.

There was no room for compromise in this choice as a decision had to be made one way or the other. There was also no way to trade off, as this was a onetime decision. The company had given Kelly two weeks to decide, and they realized that they had to make a decision in which one of them was going to be hurt or disappointed.

As they talked, they determined that Lance's need to be close to his family could be addressed by frequent flights home and Skype calls, but Kelly might never get a career opportunity like this one again. They chose to move because the need for Kelly to progress in her career outweighed the need to live in the same town as Lance's family. This type of choice involves allowing the person who is most affected to make the call.

## Is Conflict Bad?

With so many good options for making decisions, couples still end up in conflict. In fact, according to a recent study, conflict is a way of life for many couples. For example, the study found that the average couple spends forty minutes a day disagreeing and arguing over things such as household chores and money.[4]

By itself, this isn't really surprising. What is shocking is that couples reported an average of 2,455 fights a year.[5] Do the math; that's approximately seven conflicts every single day. Of course, some couples argue more or less than this, but this study shows that each day holds the potential for several conflicts between you and your partner.

The author of the study, Nikki Sellers, states, "The fact of the matter is that bickering on a daily basis is all part of being in a normal, healthy relationship." She goes on to say that "the normal co-habiting couple will have to put up with each other's daily annoyances—even if things such as housework, what to have for dinner, cleanliness and the television can prove to be very irritating."[6]

Take a look at the following list that shows the number of arguments these couples had during a year's time and what they were about. I am betting some of these are familiar to you.

| | |
|---|---|
| Not listening—112 | Overspending—109 |
| Money—108 | Laziness—105 |
| One of you snoring—102 | Bills—98 |

| | |
|---|---|
| What to eat for dinner—92 | Driving too fast—91 |
| Walking past things to go upstairs—90 | Dirty house—90 |
| What to watch on television—89 | Disciplining the children—88 |
| Dirty washing left around the house—88 | When to have sex—87 |
| Taking each other for granted—84 | Children's bedtime—83 |
| Getting home late from work—82 | Not taking washing out—82 |
| Getting in the way in the kitchen—82 | Treading mud into the house—80 |
| Spoiling the children—79 | Who should cook the evening meal—79 |
| Swearing in front of the children—79 | Not closing cupboard doors—79 |
| Parking the car—77 | Not answering your phone—76 |
| Failing to say please/thank you—75 | Not saying "I love you"—69[7] |

Nonetheless, world-famous marital researcher John Gottman feels that conflict is a good thing overall.

> If there's one lesson I've learned in my years of research into marital relationships—having interviewed and studied more than 200 couples over 20 years—it is that a lasting marriage results from a couple's ability to resolve the conflicts that are inevitable in any relationship. Many couples . . . believe the claim "we never fight" is a sign of marital health. But I believe we grow in our relationships by reconciling our differences. That's how we become more loving people and truly experience the fruits of marriage.[8]

Ken Johnson, a conflict mediator, agrees that conflict is not inherently bad, but argues that some types of conflict are clearly worse than others.[9]

I agree with these authors. Conflict, in and of itself, is not a bad thing. Disagreements, differences of opinion, and misunderstandings are bound to happen in any significant relationship. What is important is how we deal with them.

## Fighting Is a Choice

Things happen every day that create the need to negotiate the difficult waters of marital conflict. It is not a matter of whether we will have conflict with our spouses. As we have seen, it will happen, and if we are not careful, it will happen a lot. What matters is how we handle conflict when it occurs.

We don't wake up in the morning and say, "I want to fight today." Well, maybe some of us do, but that is another book! Most of us would rather get along with our husband or wife each day. We try hard to let things go, but every day presents a plethora of opportunities for disagreements and conflicts.

One of the biggest myths about marriage is that fights "just happen"; they are random, unpredictable events. Instead, people make a conscious, deliberate choice when they decide to turn a disagreement into a fight.

Saying that fights are inevitable makes it sound as though you might as well lie down and give up right now, but nothing could be further from the truth. If that were true, you would end up in a fight every time you had a difference of opinion, and that clearly doesn't happen. You can learn to see conflicts coming if you know what to look for, and you can make a choice to fight or not to fight.

This book will provide you with the tools you need to see where you are in the conflict process, teach you skills for handling conflict well when it happens, and help you learn that you have a choice in how you respond to conflict. Perhaps most importantly, it will teach you how to make the choice to end a conflict quickly and not make things worse.

→ **Choosing Not to Fight**

*Merriam-Webster's Collegiate Dictionary* defines *conflict* as a "fight" or a "battle."[10] The fact that we so often call a disagreement between two partners a "fight" says a lot about our perception of marital conflict. Fights have winners and losers and usually get worse as they go on, with one or both parties often getting hurt.

We even use analogies from battle when we talk about marital conflict. We talk about "winning" the fight, as if one side will conquer the other. We call making unfair statements in a conflict "hitting below the belt," and we refer to using hurtful statements as "bringing out the big guns."

Marriage can feel like a fight when couples are dividing scarce resources. They don't have enough money to buy everything they both want. There isn't enough time to do the things they both would like to do. They can either work together to share the limited resources or fight each other for their fair share.

Think about this for a moment. It doesn't take a rocket scientist to figure out that competing with your spouse to win some type of battle rarely brings you closer. If you make the choice to work as a team instead, your marriage will look radically different.

## Ten Choices That Will Change Your Marriage Forever

The big idea behind this book is that you can make choices in ten specific areas that will transform your marriage. You are in control of the conflicts that occur in your relationship. Conflicts will happen, but fights don't have to. You can make different choices.

Both of you can decide to work together as teammates instead of competing against each other to achieve your own individual goals. You can make a choice to do what your partner needs and give up what you need. You can choose to forgive your spouse even when you don't feel your partner deserves forgiveness.

Making the choice to love your partner does *not* mean:

I love you, as long as you are who I want you to be.

I love you, unless doing so is inconvenient.

I love you, as long as I can still get my way.

What saying "I choose to love you" *does* mean is that you are making a commitment to love your partner by making the ten specific choices I am outlining in this book. Making these choices will have consequences—sacrifice is a given in choosing to love your spouse. None of us can get what we want in a relationship all the time. Couples who successfully choose to love each other learn to agree to disagree and to honor and respect each other rather than live in the world of insults and anger that fighting creates.

Each chapter in this book will deal with one of these ten choices that all couples face in marriage. To help you learn to make these successful choices, clear strategies for achieving positive outcomes and making good decisions will be offered. You will learn specific skills you can practice and eventually master. An arrow has been placed in the margin alongside particular section headings to indicate where couples can make a truly transformational choice and *choose love*.

Each chapter also includes one or two exercises to complete with your partner to help you experience what it feels like to make successful choices in these areas. For each of the exercises, choose the best location, time, and circumstances to provide the greatest opportunity for success. You might choose a location that is quiet, with few distractions, like a corner booth in a restaurant or a park bench. The best times are often when you are not rushed, so mornings before work or late at night rarely work well. A relaxing breakfast or lunch may be much more effective. As for circumstances, avoid times when you are hungry, tired, or emotionally overwhelmed.

The ten choices in this book don't come out of thin air. They are based on three very powerful sources of information that I have learned from over the years. All three have contributed to identifying these ten specific strategies for success in marriage.

First, and most importantly, I have been in clinical practice in the field of psychology for more than twenty-five years. I have learned a great deal about what successful couples do in their relationships. In some cases, I observed the choices couples made that consistently led to positive results. In other cases, what they didn't do well was instructive; when they made changes in those areas, the outcome was much more positive. Over the years, I have found that these ten areas consistently lead to success in strong marriages and successful transformation in troubled relationships.

Second, in thirty-two years of marriage, I have learned what works and what doesn't work in my own relationship with my wife, Jan. Over and over again, when my wife and I base our choices on the principles presented in this book, the outcome makes our marriage stronger and healthier. In other words, I work very hard to practice what I preach.

Third, as a professor of counseling for more than twenty years, I have studied the marital relationship with great devotion. I have specifically been interested in learning from master therapists and top quality researchers in the field, applying their wisdom to my work with couples. Their influence has helped shape me as a therapist. You will see references to their theories and concepts in many places throughout this book.

## What You Need to Know about Me

All of us are on a journey, and knowing a little about a person's journey helps us understand the traveler. So, by way of introduction, let me tell you a few things about my journey.

I was fortunate to grow up in a Christian home with loving parents who gave me the opportunity to go to college and have a career as a psychologist. I have maintained that faith in God throughout my life, and you will see that in my writing as I talk about principles such as selflessness, forgiveness, and repentance. My faith in Christ is a big part of who I am, and it informs the principles I believe in.

However, this book is not another book written by a Christian to other Christians to help them be better Christians. In contrast, the ten choices in this book form a model of marriage that leads to healthy, strong, effective marriages regardless of your particular faith tradition. Some of you may want less spirituality in this book, while others may desire more, but it is my hope that these choices will prove to be valuable for everyone, regardless of where you are in your faith journey.

The stories of couples you will read about in this book are based on my experiences over the years as a psychologist, therapist, and professor. However, you should know that the names and details of the people and situations described in this book have been changed or presented in composite form in order to ensure the privacy of those with whom I have worked. Every attempt has been made to change all information that could lead to anyone, including the clients themselves, recognizing any individual portrayed in any story.

In addition, you should know that my own marriage has not been a smooth ride. We are making good choices now in the ten areas that you will read about, but that has not always been the case. As I wrote about in my first book, *The Controlling Husband*, we have had to overcome many challenges, including my own selfishness and baggage that were brought into the marriage from the past. It would be fair to say that I am not speaking to you from an ivory tower but as one who has spent a great deal of time in the trenches.

In this book, I am offering choices I have seen work and that I use myself. You can have confidence that these ten choices will make good relationships stronger and difficult relationships healthier. These ten choices provide hope that change is not only possible but absolutely achievable.

## Hope You Can Believe In

This book is all about hope. There is hope that if you have made poor choices in the past, you can change the way you do things in the future. There is hope that your relationship and your future as a couple are not at the mercy of disagreements or conflict. There is hope that the marriage you dreamed of when you said "I do" is not only possible but within your reach.

I call my private psychotherapy practice Transformational Marriage. My wife and I came up with this name for the business based on the complete transformation needed for a marriage to truly change for a lifetime. Our logo features a butterfly, as the metamorphosis of a caterpillar to a butterfly gives all of us hope that change is possible. The butterfly's journey truly exemplifies the healing and change that can occur in a marriage.

This is the good news about your marriage. It is *not* hopeless, and you are *not* helpless. Your marriage doesn't have to continue on the way it is. You can choose to start making choices that will transform your marriage. In the next few chapters, you will learn how to understand the process of what happens when you and your partner are in conflict and how to focus more on the way you treat each other than on what you disagree about.

Learning to make these choices will not be easy, nor will the potential challenges to your relationship be easy to overcome. Rome wasn't built in a day, right? The choices you have made in the past have served to keep you safe and protected in your relationship.

The hope you can believe in is that you and your partner can choose to be in control of what happens in your relationship. If you have the courage to take the journey this book will lead you on, the possibilities are endless. Reading this book with your partner, being open to feedback from each other, and choosing to become the most authentic, loving partners possible can lead to real and lasting transformation in your marriage.

*two*

---

# I Choose to Believe

Remember our discussion in the last chapter about jumping into love? Hope involves this concept of jumping also. The word actually comes from the idea of "jumping to safety," reminding us that reaching a place of refuge from danger provides us with hope.[1] I personally like the way *Merriam-Webster's Collegiate Dictionary* defines *hope*: "to expect with confidence."[2]

None of us knows what the future holds, but we spend much of our lives hoping the future will work out well. Perhaps you don't feel very hopeful when it comes to your marriage. You may not even believe change is possible; it may seem there is no way out of the situation in which you find yourself. Anger, bitterness, and frustration may have caused tunnel vision that prevents you from seeing all your options. This chapter will help open your eyes to options you may not have considered.

You may be generally satisfied with your marriage. There are some things you wish were different, but overall, you would say you are fine. If you are in this group, here is my question for you: Do you want to settle for a less-than-amazing marriage? If you do, you too may already have lost some hope. You are not completely dissatisfied, but you also aren't motivated to actively work to make your marriage the best it can be. You may find it easier to ignore issues and not rock the boat as long as it is still floating.

Truly believing change is possible—in other words, having hope—is the first step in transforming your marriage. You have to believe that things can get better in order to put in the work required to make that change become a reality. Whether you are newlyweds blissfully traveling the yellow brick road toward the Emerald City or a couple who has been married long enough to know the hidden dangers along that same road, hope is the first key to unlocking the future of your relationship.

## Choosing Hope

In my work with clients, the first thing I want to offer is hope. Therefore, even during the initial session, I attempt to create an environment that allows new clients to leave the session with at least one skill they can use afterward. For some couples, this may simply be learning how to take a time-out to stop a conflict from escalating into a fight.

You may be wondering why I consider hope a choice. Some people think you either have hope or you don't; they don't see it as a choice. Let's talk about this for a minute.

Think about the last time you faced a challenge. Maybe it was an assignment at work or an athletic competition. How important was your attitude when you faced that task? Those who succeed in business almost universally talk about the importance of confidence and belief in your own abilities.

I coached high school baseball for many years, and I can promise you that the athletes I worked with had to be able to see an image in their mind of crushing the ball out of the park or throwing the pitch in just the right place. Expectation and confidence are everything in a failure-based game like baseball.

When you were faced with that recent challenge, did you assume you would succeed? If so, that confidence was probably based on past success. If you weren't expecting success, you may very well have failed at a similar challenge before. Doubt and insecurity crept in, and you found yourself expecting to fail.

It is the same way in marriage. When you have had disagreements and weren't able to work them out well, or perhaps even had a big fight, you began to doubt your ability to resolve conflict. You have to change that mindset and begin to believe that you can succeed. I hear you out there . . . *But, Dr. Welch, do you expect us to just snap our fingers and start believing in something we haven't seen?*

Of course not, change takes time. Overcoming the effects of past failures is difficult, but it is absolutely possible. Hope truly is a choice. You can choose to expect the best out of your partner and yourself. You can choose to believe that you have the ability to resolve a conflict rather than say and do things that hurt each other.

## Achieving Small Successes

The key to overcoming past failures is to achieve small successes that build your confidence. To make hope a reality, you have to experience some "wins" as a couple. Even very small wins remind you of how great your relationship together can be.

Asia and John were similar to many couples who seek marriage counseling. Asia felt that John was too busy at work, that he expected her to not only work but also take care of the kids most of the time, and that he got mad and yelled at her when she just wanted to talk. John felt that Asia didn't appreciate how hard he worked to provide an income, that she was too sensitive, and that she always wanted to talk when he wanted to be left alone, leading him to become frustrated and raise his voice.

This couple needed to experience a win that would allow them both to be part of a small success and help them believe that change was possible. The big issues—lack of appreciation for each other, work-life balance, and sharing marital responsibilities—were too much to approach early in counseling.

However, anger management was a potential small victory. With many couples, I suggest that they focus on one issue, such as not yelling, that can be changed quickly and easily when both parties agree to the change. Asia and John made the choice not to worry about any other issues in their marriage for a couple of weeks while choosing to focus solely on not raising their voices and yelling at each other.

For that to happen, Asia had to let John take a break when he was getting frustrated, and John had to be honest and tell her when he felt that way. Both Asia and John agreed that yelling never solved anything in their relationship, and they both agreed that remaining calm would help them feel in control. This was not an earth-shattering change in their marriage, but when they made this choice and successfully stopped yelling, they gained a tremendous amount of hope in the possibility of transforming other aspects of their marriage.

## Learning to Expect Success

A big part of restoring hope is learning to expect success in your relationship rather than waiting for things to go wrong. Regardless of the amount of conflict in a relationship, couples can begin to expect failure and assume things will not go well. However, expecting success doesn't come cheap.

The price tag of restoring hope to your relationship can be expensive. It includes both increased vulnerability and expanded trust. You might have been let down before, and you want to avoid that feeling again. Expecting success involves trusting your partner and exposing yourself to disappointment, both of which can be costly choices.

Expecting failure is not without its own cost, though. When you expect your spouse to let you down because she or he has in the past, you run the risk of what psychologists call a self-fulfilling prophecy. You may get exactly what you expect because you have set the bar so low. You may also miss out on helping your spouse transform a part of their life because you don't think your partner is capable of change.

Of course, if you want things to remain as they are, you can simply keep doing what you have been doing. If you want your marriage to be better, however, you can take the risk of hoping things can be better. As you conquer some small, achievable goals, you begin to really believe that the relationship can be what you want it to be.

### → "Stop It!"

The first major choice you must make is to stop doing what has not worked in your relationship so far. Almost every couple I work with can benefit from the quote attributed to Albert Einstein and Benjamin Franklin, among others: "The definition of insanity is doing the same thing over and over again and expecting different results."

I want you to stop reading for a minute and try something. Google the search term "Bob Newhart five-minute therapy." An old video clip from Bob Newhart, a classic comedian who played a psychologist on *The Bob Newhart Show*, will come up. Watch the clip and see what you think.

Okay, did you watch it? Funny, right? I know it doesn't portray my profession in the best light, but it makes an important point. In order to make new choices in your marriage, you have to stop making the old ones. I will admit that Newhart's delivery needs some work, but the principle is sound. Stop doing what doesn't work, and start choosing to do new things that do work.

Before you say this is oversimplifying marriage, think about it. Isn't stopping what you're doing wrong the exact place where you have to start? You have to learn what doesn't work in your relationship and make a clear choice not to do that anymore. That is the one and only way you can make space to try new ways of handling problems.

Theodore Schwartz says the primary question that has plagued him over fifty years of counseling is why "otherwise mature, intelligent married people become irrational and defensive, attacking and abusing [each other] in the midst of a marital fight."[3] To prevent conflict from escalating, you have to know what is happening in your relationship, understand the process, and stop the downward cycle that has occurred in the past.

You will notice that I often talk about "process" in this book. You will learn a great deal about the differences in process and content in chapter 13. Briefly, when I refer to process, I am talking about the way the two of you interact, how you treat each other, and what happens between you that drives the behaviors you choose to display. Process focuses on how you relate to each other. Content focuses on a specific issue that you may disagree on.

Changing these patterns is easier said than done in a strong marriage, and it is that much harder in a relationship that is facing challenges. The first step is to become aware of what happens when you have a fight and what patterns you engage in. Making the choice to change this process is what psychologists call "disengagement," which is a fancy word for getting out of the fight before things get really bad.

## Recognizing Your Conflict Patterns

Some couples engage in a pattern that involves avoiding conflict based on prior experiences. Suppose your spouse does something that is hurtful to you. You want to bring it up, but the last time you brought something up, you got into a fight. The two of you just don't seem to be able to talk things out without fighting. So you let it go this time, but you still feel hurt and bury your feelings. Your spouse doesn't know they did anything wrong, but they already have a black mark in the "they don't care about me" category.

If you have had difficulty handling conflict in your relationship, try these two techniques to get a handle on what is going wrong.

First, sit down with your partner and write down the steps that took place in the last big argument you had. Write down when one of you first got upset, who it was, and why. Then write down what happened next, how you each reacted, how that led to things getting worse, and so on.

You are creating a time line for the argument that includes each comment, behavior, or emotion that led to the next step. Don't leave anything out—every aspect of the argument is important. Write down how you felt and what you experienced at each step in the process all the way to the end.

After you have written out the story, talk about what you have written. When did things specifically start to go wrong? Can you pinpoint the actual start of the argument, or did you both enter the discussion ready to fight (perhaps because a previous conflict had never been resolved)? Did certain things escalate the conflict and make things worse? Perhaps most importantly, talk about whether there is a pattern of how you handle conflict that happens fairly regularly.

Second, make a list of some of the things that contribute to the conflicts you have. What are the hot topics you try to avoid? Maybe you can identify the time of day that is the most problematic for you to discuss an issue, or perhaps there is a certain attitude or tone of voice that really frustrates one or both of you. Do common factors or experiences repeat themselves? Hopefully you can see things that contribute to how you handle conflict as a couple that provide insight into why things don't go well.

Try to learn as much from each other as you can about the process that occurs when you disagree. You both have to agree on what times and places do and don't work for serious discussions and what land mines to avoid in the process. The long-term goal is to become good at knowing when you are beginning a fight and seeing a fight coming.

## Are You Ready for Some Wins?

I began this chapter by suggesting that hope grows in a marriage when you have small successes. These small wins are like planting a seed and carefully nurturing it as it grows. Many years ago, Bill Murray played the title role in the movie *What About Bob?* Richard Dreyfuss played Dr. Leo Marvin, a psychotherapist who wrote a book titled *Baby Steps*. In the book, he wrote that change needs to occur in "small, reasonable goals that you set for yourself one day at a time."

Now, it is true that Dr. Marvin's patient, Bob, becomes so obsessed with him that he shows up at his lake house while he is on vacation with his family! So we won't talk about that part of the story line. The point is that these "baby steps" are really the key to restoring hope in a marriage.

Trust isn't built overnight, and you won't immediately change all the problematic conflict patterns you have developed. You need to have small, reasonable goals that you can achieve as a couple. For example, if you have had difficulty remaining calm during disagreements, you could make the same choice Asia and John did and decide not to raise your voices during arguments. If your marriage has fallen into a pattern of negativity and resentment, you could choose to make one positive comment to each other every day or do one chore around the house you don't usually do.

The idea is to come up with some things you can change in your relationship and then celebrate the wins when you succeed. These will help you remember that the two of you can work together as a team and will foster the growth of hope.

### EXERCISE
### Learning to Take Baby Steps

In almost every chapter of this book, you will find exercises like this one. For the process of transformation to work, you *must* do these exercises. I strongly recommend that you look at the book as a series of steps. When you see the heart illustration, that is your cue to stop reading and to take the time to complete the exercise as a couple. Think of these exercises as a workbook within a book.

#### Baby Step 1: Remembering the Good Times

To build hope in your relationship, you have to create a soft bed to land on to cushion the fall when conflict occurs. That means remembering the good times—when you were dating, when you fell in love, the wedding, the honeymoon, and all the other good memories that your relationship includes. (I am making an assumption that the honeymoon was actually a good memory for you, although I know that is not always the case.)

Think back to why you fell in love. Forgive the clichés, but do you remember when he seemed to be your knight in shining armor? And when she was the angel that fell from the sky? I have no idea how fresh those feelings are for both of you, but it is incredibly important that you stay in touch with them.

Jan and I celebrate our anniversary every month, even after more than thirty years. It is our way of reminding ourselves more than once a year how glad we are that we found each other. We use these anniversaries to remember the many great memories and inside stories we share, and they give us current positive experiences to balance the negative.

Years ago, we received some small Chick-fil-A cows in one of their promotions. Jan decided to surprise me with one and hid it in my shoe to let me know she was thinking of me. What started out as a cute joke is now a "thing." I have found Chick-fil-A cows in my luggage and underneath my pillow, and Jan has found them at her school and in her purse. It is our way of saying "I love you" when we are not there.

So here is the exercise. Write down, individually, your memories of good times in your relationship. Identify at least five of the best times you recall in your marriage. Be specific—write down exactly what happened and why you enjoyed being married to your partner at that time. Write down how you felt and why you felt that way.

Once you have each made your list, share them with each other. Again, be specific. Tell your spouse why you enjoyed that time so much and what about the experience made you appreciate being married in that moment.

If you want to take this to the next level, make scrapbooks or albums of these experiences. When times get rough, you can pull one out and remind yourselves of the good times you have had together.

### *Baby Step 2: A Small Success*

After you have completed the first step, you can move on to this second assignment. Choose an issue that has caused disagreement between the two of you. It should be a topic that doesn't have huge consequences for either of you; look for a problem that you might be able to work out a solution to. Don't worry—you will have plenty of time later to deal with the big stuff! For now, the goal is simply to succeed, and for that, you need a target you can actually hit.

Once you pick the issue, choose a time and a place to discuss it. This is not as easy as you might think. Couples often set themselves up for failure by picking a time when they are both tired or a location that has too many distractions. Remember, your goal is to successfully address this issue, so make that as likely as possible.

Once you have chosen a topic, a time, and a place, make a commitment not to cancel the appointment. Put the same high priority on this meeting as you would a lunch with an important business contact or a close friend. Your goal during this time is to make sure you each listen carefully to what the other is saying.

Here is the key. I mentioned earlier that the goal is to successfully address this issue. That does *not* mean one of you has to win! You don't even have to end up making a decision. If you both listen carefully to each other, get all the opinions out on the table, and make sure both voices are clearly heard, *that's* a win. If you actually come up with a solution that works, that is just icing on the cake.

## The Choice to Believe

So how do you feel? You have just taken the initial steps toward transforming your marriage. You will have to practice these baby steps to get better at succeeding. Don't expect to be 100 percent successful, but make a commitment to believe change is possible in your relationship and to expect the best from your partner.

If hope is expecting success with confidence, as we discussed earlier, then you should feel a bit more hopeful right now. You should believe that you can choose to make your relationship what you have always hoped it would be. This choice to believe transformation is possible will set the stage for real change in your marriage.

Hope will lead you where you want to go on the journey. Taking these baby steps—remembering the good times and setting and succeeding at small goals—can allow love to grow in the hope that healing is possible. Asia and John found that as they celebrated small successes, hope returned to their relationship. Like picking low-hanging fruit, making a decision to set small goals for improving your relationship isn't that hard.

Hope is extremely contagious. When you choose to believe in your future, you send the message to your partner that you believe in them. This choice sets the stage for every other choice offered in this book. When you stop expecting failure and choose to believe in each other, you will begin to understand why hope is so central to transforming your relationship.

# *three*

# I Choose to Communicate Well

## Part 1: *Choosing to Communicate Accurately*

When was the last time someone listened to you? No, I don't mean they heard what you said. I mean the person stopped everything they were doing, focused on what you had to say, looked in your eyes, and really *listened* so that you came away from the conversation thinking, *Wow, they really got me!*

This kind of listening doesn't happen often. In our fast-paced, high-pressure world, we rarely slow down enough to really listen to those around us. Did you know that most people listen to only about the first quarter to one half of what another person is saying before they lose focus and start thinking about what they plan to say in response?[1] You can't thoughtfully respond to someone when you haven't heard all of what they have said. And frankly, not listening well makes it more likely your partner won't bother to share with you in the future.

Here is another question. When was the last time you spoke clearly and concisely and said exactly what you meant in the briefest manner possible? If you want your partner to listen to you well, you have to speak well. Much of the time it almost seems that we are speaking to hear ourselves talk rather than really saying exactly what we mean.

The big idea in this chapter is that communication is not a spectator sport. It is an ongoing, two-way interaction that occurs effectively only when both partners are committed to paying attention and understanding each other. It involves speaking and listening, verbal and nonverbal actions, and thoughts and emotions. Communication is hard work! In this chapter, you will find specific exercises to help you become skilled at both speaking and listening.

## The ABCs of Transformational Communication

In my years working with couples, I have discovered four secrets to communicating well:

1. Active listening—listening well and verifying the message
2. Brevity—speaking in brief bullet points
3. Clarity—making clear, easy-to-understand statements
4. Delivery—delivering the message with the proper tone and attitude

### Active Listening

How do you know that your partner understood what you said? Most people just assume the other person understood, and that is a dangerous assumption to make. This is where accuracy and verification come in. You have to be absolutely certain that your partner understood what you wanted them to hear.

## EXERCISE
## Learning to Listen Well

We can all agree that it is great when your partner understands you and gets what you are saying. This may not happen as often as you would like, but when it does, you both feel a tremendous amount of hope for the future of the relationship. You feel listened to and understood, and it feels really good. How can you make sure this happens more often in your marriage?

Harville Hendrix's book *Getting the Love You Want* is now in a twentieth anniversary edition.[2] I don't necessarily agree with his theory on how couples can "get the love they want," but I do highly value the exercises in active listening he offers in the book. I saw him demonstrate these skills at a seminar a few years back. The principles are solid and incredibly effective.

You have probably heard of the basic idea behind active listening, which at its core involves restating what you believe your partner said and meant. Hendrix takes this idea and expands on it to give you a step-by-step process that virtually guarantees you will understand each other with amazing clarity and accuracy.

What follows is an example of how this works, based on the process Hendrix presents in his book. For this example, we will assume the wife has an issue that she wants to talk about with her husband. First, she describes her thoughts and feelings about the issue to her husband.

Next, the husband mirrors back what his wife said, as accurately as possible, by stating, "If I got it right, you said . . . Did I get it right?"

If she says yes, the husband says, "Is there more I need to know?" and she can share her additional thoughts, with the husband mirroring those back until he gets it right. If she says no, then the wife clarifies what is incorrect and she communicates her thoughts again until they are received correctly.

Then the husband summarizes by saying, "Let me see if I got all of that. I believe you said . . . Did I get it all?" If the wife says yes, then they can move on. If not, she continues to clarify until the husband gets it correctly.

Hendrix suggests that the husband could take two more steps. He can validate his wife by saying, "I get what you are saying, because . . ." and then stating why what she said makes sense to him. He does *not* have to agree, but simply state that he understands. He can also offer empathy by saying, "I can imagine that you might be feeling . . ." to help show that he understands the emotion that goes with her words.

It is important to understand that this exercise is not a two-way process. The person who is listening does *not* get to argue back, say what they think about what their partner is saying, or make any judgmental or reactive comments. The only role of the listener is to listen. If they would like to ask to share their thoughts in a later conversation, they can do so. They just cannot share their thoughts now.

I cannot tell you how valuable this process is in producing accurate, clear communication. Once the first partner has heard and understood accurately, then the couple can choose to flip roles and repeat the process. It often helps to separate each person's turn in sharing so that both parties feel they are heard and respected.

### Brevity

Brevity matters in communication. As I mentioned earlier, we often listen to only half or less of what others are saying before we lose focus. If we want our partners to hear us, we can't give a speech; we have to keep it simple.

I see this every week in my counseling practice. When a wife (or it could be a husband) shares her opinion, she lists every reason she can think of to support her point. Her husband usually responds in one of two ways: he is either overwhelmed with all the information or loses focus because there are too many facts to process.

Think of it this way. If you have a valid point, why complicate your communication by saying it twelve ways? Just make the point and wait for a response. Let your partner clearly hear and understand the main point and respond in kind.

I have developed an exercise for my clients that helps them learn this skill. It can also help you learn to communicate with brevity in an effective manner.

### EXERCISE
## Using Bullet-Point Statements

For this exercise, you and your partner need to set aside about an hour. You will be working on communicating well, so choose a place that is comfortable for both of you and free from distractions. You will have plenty of opportunities in the future to practice these skills in less than ideal circumstances.

First, choose a topic that one of you would like to talk to the other about. Don't make the topic extremely controversial; remember, you want to work primarily on learning the skill. It doesn't matter who goes first; each of you will have an opportunity to choose a topic.

Second, think about exactly what you want to say to the other person before you speak.

Third, talk in bullet points. State what you want to say in simple sentences that form clear bullet-point statements. Focus on the specific information you want your partner to know and avoid any irrelevant information.

Here is an example of a poor bullet-point statement: "I have thought for a long time that there are so many things I am upset about, and I just don't know how to tell you because when I try to tell you things, you don't really listen, and when you come home late or you are in a bad mood when you are watching football and your team loses . . . it's just all so unfair."

Here is an example of a good bullet-point statement: "When you come home late more than three nights each week, I feel that you don't want to spend time with me."

Fourth, once you have made the statement, ask your partner, "Could I have said that just as accurately in a shorter bullet-point statement?" Remember, this is not the time to debate the topic but simply to get feedback from your partner.

Once the first partner has completed the exercise, switch roles and have the other partner complete the same steps. Do this exercise three to four times with different topics so that you can practice speaking in bullet points. When you have completed this exercise, share any observations or suggestions you each have on how you can use this skill in your relationship. Practice this when you speak in meetings at work or with your friends. You will be amazed at the effect it has on others' understanding of what you are saying. Isn't this the desire we all have—to be understood when we speak?

### *Clarity*

One couple I worked with opened a session with the following interchange:

Camila: When you use that tone of voice, there's no point in talking to you.

Luis: What tone of voice?

Camila: You know the one!

Luis: No. If I did, I wouldn't ask you. You always say I have a tone, but I have no idea what you are talking about.

Camila: That's because you never listen to me. You just yell at me.

Luis: I don't yell at you! That's not fair. I barely raise my voice and you say I'm yelling. I can't win.

Camila: This is why I don't talk to you. You won't listen to me. I'm telling you exactly what I want you to stop doing, and you don't even care.

Luis: I just don't know how to do what you want when I don't even understand what you are saying.

Dr. Welch: Camila, could you give Luis an example of when he last used a tone with you or yelled at you?

48

Camila: I don't know. He does it all the time. It's how he always talks to me.

Dr. Welch: Do you remember when we talked about how using words like "all" and "never" make it hard to accurately communicate? He doesn't seem to always use a tone of voice or yell at you during our sessions, right?

Camila: Well, no. It just feels like it is all the time. He calms down when he comes in here because he's in front of you. He puts on his best face.

Luis: (sighing) I do not. That's so unfair.

Camila: (looking at Luis) You don't even have to raise your voice. The tone says you're mad or frustrated, and if we talk at all, you are short and dismissive. (turning to me) Can you help us? This is why we're here. He never listens to me.

Camila believed they were struggling with a listening problem, but it was actually more of a communication issue. Listening problems are often communication problems in disguise. In this case, there was a problem with clarity. Camila was trying to express to Luis that both raising his voice and the tone of voice he used made her feel unheard and unloved. Luis could not understand what she was trying to say.

Clarity is a measure of how accurately the message you sent was received by your partner. Camila used several terms, including "tone" and "yelling," to try to help Luis understand, but it didn't work. She needed to be much clearer and more specific in what she was asking for.

The key to this skill is thinking about what you want to say before you say it. This takes some work, as most of us are used to speaking off the cuff without considering our words. To speak with clarity, you must consider your words, think about how your partner will hear them, and say exactly what you mean to say. This is hard to do when you are angry, as you may find yourself saying things you will regret. If you are too angry to think about your words, you should not be having a discussion with your partner. Take time to cool off first.

Your statements to your partner must be crystal clear in order to be effective—thus, the importance of clarity in communication. An example would be, "Luis, when you use a joking, sarcastic tone after I say something important, it feels like you don't take me seriously and don't value my opinion." That tells Luis in a clear manner that Camila is asking him to change a specific tone of voice that makes her uncomfortable.

I worked with Luis to help him understand what Camila was asking him to change about his tone. She told him that the sarcastic and condescending tone he used had hurt her feelings and made her feel disrespected and unappreciated. It wasn't until Camila gave him specific, clear examples of what his words sounded like to her that he started to understand.

More importantly, we did some reverse role playing in which Camila took the part of Luis and spoke in the tone she heard from him. He started to understand the impact of his comments when he saw himself through his wife's eyes. However, even when Luis *did* monitor his tone and did not raise his voice, Camila sometimes did not notice his efforts due to her expectation of his failure. It takes time and solid effort from both partners to change these patterns.

One final thought regarding clarity and brevity. You have to give up some power to communicate in this manner. You can't be focused on winning an argument or proving your point—those goals are mutually exclusive to communicating well.

Do you want to "win" or be understood? If your goal is to be understood, then getting your way in the discussion is irrelevant. This may be an entirely new concept for both of you, and we will explore concepts such as selflessness and sacrifice later in this book. For now, I just want you to consider that how you feel about each other after you discuss an issue may be more important than the outcome of the discussion.

### Delivery

If you want your partner to be open to what you have to say, pay attention to how you say it. In other words, it's all about the delivery. The tone you use, the attitude you present, and the context in which you present your words all affect the way your message is heard.

Many of us can recognize a tone of voice clearly when others use it, but we don't hear it in our own voices when we speak. It is very important that you and your partner learn to recognize negative, destructive tones of voice in yourself and each other so that you can stop using them.

### Five Tones to Avoid

I have identified five destructive tones of voice that people use. Each tone has distinctive characteristics that hurt people in specific ways. To understand them, it may help to hear what they sound like in a conflict between a fictional husband and wife. In the interaction that follows, you will encounter the five tones of voice. Notice that each tone is increasingly destructive and damaging.

*Distrustful tone.* Julie and Dwayne are having a discussion about their finances. Money was always a little challenging to talk about, as they had limited resources and different ways of managing money. Julie paid one bill late and paid the wrong amount on another, and Dwayne found out about it. Julie told him that she had lost one bill but paid it when she found it, while she had paid the original amount on the other.

Dwayne starts the conversation by saying, "Let me get this straight. You want me to believe that you *lost* one bill and the other bill wasn't correct? That's the story you're going with? I really can't trust you to do anything, can I?"

Can you hear the questioning in Dwayne's response? He flat-out doesn't believe Julie and thinks she is making up an excuse. He has a pessimistic attitude and assumes she is trying to get out of accepting responsibility for her mistake. The possibility that she was being honest, had tried to handle the problem the best she could, and that the problem was not Julie's fault did not even enter Dwayne's mind.

Julie responds by saying, "You think I'm lying? I wouldn't do that. I'm just explaining what happened. You're not listening to me."

*Critical tone.* Dwayne laughs derisively at her and makes a comment as he begins to walk out of the room. "You know what my expectation is. You pay the bills on time and don't make mistakes." With that, Dwayne stomps out of the room.

Dwayne's comment here is both disrespectful and corrective at the same time. He uses a very authoritarian tone that indicates the argument is over and he is done communicating with his wife. This final comment sounds more like a father talking to a child than a husband to his wife, as he addresses her as a second-class citizen.

*Condescending tone.* As he often does, after stomping out of the room, Dwayne returns to continue his tirade. "I think it's time we face the fact that you just aren't capable of handling money. I guess I have to lower the bar even further. I will have to stop expecting you to ever do it right. It's clear that I just need to pay the bills myself."

Do you see the sarcasm in what Dwayne says? He is being contemptuous and talking down to Julie, but perhaps more importantly, he is shaming her in the process. Dwayne manages to make Julie feel like a failure, and at the same time, he makes it clear how much better he could have handled the situation.

*Dismissive tone.* Julie makes one more attempt to explain that one bill got lost in her purse, but she paid it as soon as she found it. Getting no response from Dwayne, she goes on to say that she actually paid the amount that was indicated on the other bill, but that some additional charges were added that hadn't been on the original bill.

Dwayne responds, "Whatever. Just forget about it. It's not even worth talking to you about it. I don't know why I bother." He turns away and starts looking at his phone.

Now Dwayne is completely ignoring what Julie says. He is indifferent to information she presents and responds in a curt manner. In effect, he dismisses her response and doesn't even acknowledge her.

Julie says, "I don't know how to talk to you when you get like this. There's nothing I can say to keep you from being angry and hurtful."

*Aggressive tone.* "Seriously?" Dwayne retorts, beginning to raise his voice. "You are going to try to turn this around and blame me? Don't even go there." Almost shouting at this point, Dwayne says, "This is your fault, and I am sick and tired of you blaming me for your mistakes. You need to stop that right now!"

Dwayne has now escalated the conflict to a full-blown fight. He is loud, angry, and aggressive, and his tone has become biting, threatening, and intimidating. He is trying to manipulate Julie and force her to give in to his point of view.

At this point, Julie gives up. She knows she won't win a shouting match, and frankly, she doesn't have the energy to fight back. She considers a sarcastic retort but realizes it will just make Dwayne angrier. She meekly responds with an "I'm sorry. I didn't mean to make you mad." Dwayne stalks out of the room, and as Julie begins to cry, she thinks, *I don't know how much more of this I can take.*

### Changing the Delivery

Changing your tone of voice is really just a matter of delivering your message in a new way. Each of Dwayne's statements could be rephrased to deliver a message that is just as accurate and truthful but not hurtful, destructive, or demeaning. Here are some examples.

*Distrustful tone.* Dwayne said to Julie, "Let me get this straight. You want me to believe that you *lost* one bill and the other bill wasn't correct? That's the story you're going with? I really can't trust you to do anything, can I?"

To reframe this statement, Dwayne could eliminate the sarcastic elements "Let me get this straight" and "That's the story you're going with?" He could also eliminate the hurtful statement "I really can't trust you to do anything, can I?" These statements serve no purpose other than to guarantee that Julie will not hear what he wants to share, as she will focus on the feelings of disrespect these statements create.

That leaves the real bullet point of the message, which is that Dwayne doesn't trust Julie to tell the truth. He could say, "I want to be honest with you. In the past, I've had difficulty trusting you, and I feel that same way now. Can you help me understand how you lost one bill and what happened with the other bill?"

*Critical tone.* Dwayne said, "You know what my expectation is. You pay the bills on time and don't make mistakes." This statement creates a power differential in the marriage. To sound less critical and condemning, Dwayne could say, "It's hard for me when we don't pay bills on time. I understand mistakes sometimes happen, so would you be comfortable letting me know when there is an issue with a lost bill or you are confused by how much needs to be paid?"

*Condescending tone.* Dwayne said, "I think it's time we face the fact that you just aren't capable of handling money. I guess I have to lower the bar even further. I will have to stop expecting you to ever do it right." Any statement that includes absolutes or judgments is likely to feel condescending to your partner. Again, if Dwayne wants Julie to actually hear what he has to say, he should eliminate comments such as "You just aren't capable" and "I guess I have to lower the bar."

It would be much more helpful and effective to say "I appreciate the fact that you have been taking care of the bills. I know that's a lot of work. How can I help you with this task?" This approach eliminates the condescending, contemptuous tone of voice and focuses on the need to work together as a team to complete the tasks that are necessary in a marriage.

*Dismissive tone.* When a couple progresses in intensity to a dismissive tone of voice, it becomes more likely that communication will be negative or end altogether. Dwayne responded to Julie's explanation of the situation by saying, "Whatever. Just forget about it. It's not worth even talking to you about it. I don't know why I bother." This statement is tough to rephrase because, at its core, it is really an attempt to end the conversation. However, it would be honest and potentially helpful to say, "I'm really getting frustrated right now, and I'm not sure I can listen very well. Why don't we take a time-out and talk about this again tomorrow?" This would allow Dwayne to honestly tell Julie how he is feeling without terminating all discussion or continuing with a negative and hurtful interaction.

*Aggressive tone.* The final and most destructive tone of voice often leads to what amounts to verbal abuse. For the most part, this tone of voice should be avoided completely. Dwayne's following statement is hard to state in a positive light. Listen again to what he said. "Seriously? You are going to try to turn this around and blame me? Don't even go there. This is your fault, and I am sick and tired of you blaming me for your mistakes. You need to stop that right now!"

Realistically, the best choice for Dwayne in this situation would be to simply stop making aggressive statements altogether. If you are at this point in an argument, it is best to take some time away from the discussion and reengage at a later time. In chapter 5, you will learn a specific skill set for taking a time-out and disengaging from a negative, destructive communication process.

## The Choice to Communicate Accurately

You may not be in a relationship with someone as hurtful as Dwayne, but now that you know these five tones of voice, you will be aware of the destruction they can cause. These tones don't occur by accident—you make a conscious choice to use them against your spouse. If you make the choice to be distrustful, critical, condescending, dismissive, or aggressive with your partner, don't be surprised if the damage you do has long-lasting consequences.

The ABCs of transformational communication will help you and your spouse communicate both clearly and accurately. When you increase active listening, maximize brief and clear messages, and choose to deliver the messages without destructive tones, both of your voices will be heard. You will also have a much better chance of knowing what you each think and feel.

When you choose to speak in ways your partner can hear and listen to each other carefully, you show each other respect and dignity. I grew up in a family with values based on faith, and one of those values that is still vitally important to me today is showing respect for others. If you choose to listen first and save your counterarguments for a later time, your partner will feel valued and cared for. Treating your partner with dignity isn't just about successful communication—it is the right thing to do.

*four*

# I Choose to Communicate Well

*Part 2: Choosing to Communicate Positively*

John Gottman has conducted research on thousands of couples in his career. One constant he has found is that it takes at least five positive statements to make up for one negative statement. He calls this his Magic Rule of 5:1. In fact, Gottman believes that praise is one thing that can keep criticism from turning into contempt, defensiveness, and stonewalling.[1]

Think about how this works in your marital relationship. Do you spend more time telling your spouse what they have done wrong or what they have done right? If you have corrected or criticized your spouse in three or four ways before you have even had lunch, Gottman would say you now need to say fifteen to twenty positive things to make up for it. That should make you think twice the next time you want to make a critical comment!

This chapter is about choosing to encourage and build each other up in positive ways. You are more than likely the most important human voice your partner listens to. If the most important person in your life—your marital partner—is a negative influence on you, the result could be low self-esteem, depression, or self-destructiveness. It is imperative that you are a strong, positive, uplifting presence in the life of your partner.

## Positive Praise

On the surface, it would seem obvious that praise is one of the most positive things we can do for our partners. Unfortunately, praise doesn't always end up being a positive experience. I have often heard a wife or husband respond to a partner's praise by saying, "That's nice, but you have to say that since we're married." At other times, praise is not valued because it doesn't outweigh the negative criticism that has occurred previously.

Almost everyone would agree that praise is incredibly important to children for their self-esteem and development. Somehow, we forget this lesson when it comes to our marriages. We don't lose the need for self-confidence and self-worth just because we become adults and get married. Our partners are, or should be, a valuable source of positive feedback for us.

Hearing positive messages from the person whose opinion matters most to us is extremely important. By the same token, if we hear criticism from the person who is supposed to love and accept us, it hurts all that much more. However, for many couples, positive praise proves to be something that is *simple* but not *easy*.

A marriage characterized by criticism and complaints has a great deal of negativity. Communication is most often focused on what is wrong in the relationship due to hurt, anger, bitterness, or poor conflict resolution. Imagine if this was turned around into a marriage founded on praise and encouragement. I have watched this amazing transformation in the couples I work with.

One resource to consider using is the book *The 5 Love Languages* by Gary Chapman.[2] Chapman argues that if we understand the communication styles that each of us use to send and receive messages, we can have much more positive interactions in our marriages. Many couples find that this book helps them understand each other's needs and how to communicate well with each other.

To get a feel for what positive interactions in relationships can look like, let's take a look at some examples from business and coaching. Leaders in business and athletics provide insight into the damage that negative feedback can create and, in contrast, the transformation that positive feedback can provide.

## Positive Leadership

Researchers have expanded on the important research of John Gottman described earlier in this chapter on positive behavior. In studying business leadership teams, researchers indicated that the number one factor in leadership success was the ratio of positive to negative comments. In contrast to Gottman's research, which focused on the negative effects of criticism, these studies focused on the positive effects of praise. The top leadership teams averaged five to six positive comments for every negative one, while the low-performing teams averaged three negative comments for every positive one.[3]

There is an online quiz to determine what is called the "Happiness Ratio." This is certainly not a clinical test, but it may help you get a feel for how much positivity you currently have in your life. The quiz can be found at http://happier human.com/positivity-ratio/.[4] You can both take the quiz to compare levels of positivity in your lives.

For many of us, the feedback we receive at our jobs forms the basis for whether our days go well. We spend forty to sixty hours (or more) at our jobs every week, which is much more time than most married couples spend together each week. Sometimes having a bad day at work can create conflict in our marriages. If we are not careful, receiving negative feedback at work can become a template for how we treat our spouses.

## Positive Coaching

I have been a coach for over twenty years, from the highest competitive levels of youth sports to high school baseball and basketball. In addition, I have served for many years as a consultant to high-level college sports teams, working with NCAA athletes, coaching staffs, and administrators. These various perspectives have taught me a great deal about the differences between positive and negative coaching.

Athletes are motivated in many ways; some need to be pressed to play to their potential, while others need softer encouragement. Coaches have a variety of approaches for providing this motivation. From the iconic Bobby Knight, who is perhaps known best for throwing a chair across a basketball court, to the legendary Phil Jackson, known for a calm, Zen-like mental approach to coaching, each leader chooses a different motivational style.

The NCAA says that out of eight million students who play high school sports, only about five hundred thousand will make a college team.[5] Many young athletes will be coached with negative, fear-based strategies by coaches who yell incredibly obvious things at nine- and ten-year-old players such as "throw strikes" and "kick it in the goal."

I have certainly made the mistake of using negative coaching at times in my own coaching career. What I have come to believe is that negative coaching that breaks players down does not work the way coaches think it does. Players may want to avoid a coach yelling at them or pulling them out of the game, but they are playing out of fear. Players rarely play well when they are afraid of making mistakes.

In my work with athletes and coaches, both as a coach and as a consultant, I try to focus consistently on providing feedback to athletes in a manner that is motivational and encouraging. If an athlete makes a mistake, chances are they are well aware of what they did wrong. They don't need a coach to repeat that fact. What they do need, as my younger son's coaches taught him, is to admit the mistake and not repeat it.

## Positive Coaching and Marriage

You may be wondering how coaching relates to marriage; allow me to explain. If you are in a relationship with someone who chooses to criticize you, you likely live in fear of making mistakes or getting "in trouble." In contrast, if your partner builds you up by letting mistakes go, focusing on the future, and encouraging you with praise, you expect that the future will be bright and positive. Rather than waiting for something to go wrong, you may take more chances to give the relationship the opportunity to grow and flourish.

Just like the young soccer goalie who has to forget that she just allowed a goal and get right back to stopping the next one, marriage partners must learn from mistakes, forgive each other, and move forward. We will make mistakes, and we will hurt each other's feelings; what matters is that we learn from these choices and make different ones in the future.

I see the same things happening in marriages that I see in athletics. When we are truly teammates who support and pick each other up, even when one of us has let the other down, we can make it through the hard times. Any couple or athlete can thrive when they are winning; the key is how they react when times get tough and they are down by two touchdowns in the second half.

## Positive Communication

Replacing negative communication with positive communication can literally transform marriages. To help you make this choice in your marriage, I have developed a set of rules that focus on being positive when you are communicating with each other. Using these rules won't prevent you from disagreeing or having differences of opinions. What you *can* prevent are the hurtful fights in which you say things you regret. There is no reason you ever have to fight like that again.

Changing how you speak to each other, when you speak to each other, and where you speak to each other are important. Focusing on how you both feel rather than winning the argument and listening to your partner so that you truly understand what they want you to know are equally valuable choices. These choices can prevent the anger and resentment so many couples experience.

In the past, authors have presented rules for fighting fairly in conflicts, but I think doing so completely misses the point. Couples will have disagreements, but I don't want you to "fight fair." I want you not to fight at all! You know how to fight, and it never ends well. If you follow my ten rules for positive communication, you will significantly decrease the likelihood that disagreements will turn into fights you will both regret later.

 ### *10 Rules for Positive Communication*

#### Rule 1: Don't Bring Up the Past

Bringing up past conflicts confuses the issue and changes the subject.

Old emotions from previous conflicts get brought in.

When old emotions are brought in, the conversation can quickly turn negative.

*Positive communication focuses on what is currently happening.*

#### Rule 2: Deal with One Conflict at a Time

Stick with the issue at hand and don't get sidetracked.

Bringing in other issues just muddies the waters.

64

If one partner brings up a different issue, the other should point that out and redirect them to the primary issue.

*Positive communication focuses on one clear issue at a time.*

### Rule 3: Don't Deal with Problems Late at Night

No one ever resolves a problem well after 10:00 p.m. . . . period.

Both partners are tired from the day.

The brain doesn't function well late at night, and you aren't thinking clearly.

The chances of a conflict escalating are sky high.

Unless it is truly an emergency discussion, save it for the morning.

*Positive communication occurs when both parties have good energy, clarity, and focus.*

### Rule 4: Don't Deal with Problems When Short on Time

Don't start something that can't be finished.

If rushed, you won't listen well.

Communication is likely to be negative, and one or both of you will feel unheard.

*Positive communication occurs when there is enough time and both parties are prepared to have a healthy discussion about the issue.*

### Rule 5: Tell the Truth; Hiding Things Doesn't Help

Grandmother was right—honesty is the best policy.

Once the first lie is told, you have to keep telling more to
maintain the story.

More importantly, once your partner stops trusting you
because you lied or hid things, earning back their trust
is difficult.

*Positive communication is authentic, honest, truthful, and
transparent.*

### Rule 6: Don't Hit below the Belt

Choose not to use the words or emotions you know will
hit your partner where it really hurts.

Don't say hurtful, unkind words; you'll only have to apologize later.

*Positive communication is constructive—not destructive.*

### Rule 7: Focus on What Will Work in the Future instead of What Went Wrong in the Past

Having the same argument repeatedly isn't helpful.

Unfinished business from the past will have to be dealt
with at some point—just not now.

Focusing on the past prevents you from moving forward.
Look forward to making things different in the future.

*Positive communication creates solutions to current problems.*

### Rule 8: Listen More Than You Talk

When all else fails, be quiet. Better yet, lead with listening.

You will be surprised how much you learn when you listen.

More importantly, your partner will feel heard and loved.

One partner should listen first, clearly reflect what they understood, and wait for confirmation that they got it right before the conversation proceeds.

*Positive communication occurs when one partner shares and one partner listens.*

### Rule 9: Use Bullet Points

Say only what needs to be said and no more.

Speak in clear, easily understandable bullet-point statements.

*Positive communication is clear, direct, and easy to understand.*

### Rule 10: Avoid Destructive, Hurtful Statements

If a comment will be insulting or hurtful, don't make it.

Rethink the language you plan to use, and reword the statement in a constructive way.

If communication is turning negative, interrupt the process and disengage for a time.

Return to the discussion when it can be positive.

*Positive and negative communication are mutually exclusive.*

Try these ten rules for positive communication the next time you need to discuss something with your spouse. These rules are effective not just for conflict resolution but for any interaction you have. You will find that daily communication about everything improves if you follow these ten rules.

## Positive Cooperation

Choosing to be positive in your relationship involves more than communication. Couples who function from a positive mind-set are more cooperative than competitive. When the relationship becomes competitive, it has likely also turned negative.

There are always scarce resources in a marriage. No one has an unending supply of things such as time, money, patience, love, and kindness. If partners work together as teammates to develop and share the resources available, the relationship is strengthened. However, if they become jealous or resentful and try to get their fair share of the scarce resources, things quickly become negative and competitive. The marriage begins to look like *The Hunger Games* or an episode of *Survivor*, with only one winner.

This competition over scarce resources is one of the biggest challenges couples face. One partner may truly believe that since there is not enough for both parties to get everything they want they must fight to get their needs met. In this type of competition, there really is no winner. The end result is often pain, despair, isolation, or divorce.

In contrast, a healthy marriage is a cooperative venture in which both partners try to help each other become the best people and the best spouses they can be. The goal is not to win by ending up with more of the limited resources in the relationship, but to make sure that each partner is loved, accepted, valued, and honored in their interactions.

## Positive Joy

One of the most positive things we can do for our marriages is to laugh together and enjoy each other's company. A positive marriage is a fun marriage. We need to make time for fun. This may sound like simple advice, but with busy schedules, finding the time can be tougher than it sounds.

When do you have fun in your relationship? Some of you may live for the weekend because the week is full of work and kids' activities, but then you find that the weekend is full of more of the same. Others of you may live for vacations, enjoying two weeks away from your normal life, but then become frustrated and disappointed when the same problems and challenges greet you when you return.

Where do you find joy, peace, contentment, and rest in your daily life? Your marriage should be a place of safety and security in which you know each other well enough to share laughter and joy on a regular basis. If you don't have that type of joy in your marriage, you can make the choice to change.

Why do we not experience joy in our marriages? For some, conflict and stress may take up all the energy in the relationship. There are many chapters in this book that provide tools to address these struggles. It may be that decreasing conflict will provide the space for joy in your marriage.

Others may be so busy that there is simply not enough time to enjoy each other. That problem is fairly easy to fix. Marriage is about choices. If you want to spend more time with your spouse, you may need to spend less time at the office, and that may mean you don't get the next big promotion. You have a choice to make.

Still others reading this may have let any number of other choices interfere with their joy. Difficulties with communication, forgiveness, selfishness, "unspoken truths," intimacy, trust, relating to each other, or taking each other for granted may have led to a lack of joy in your marriage. It is my sincere hope that this book will unlock some of these chains, allowing you to pursue joy and peace in your marriage.

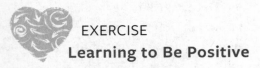

## EXERCISE
## Learning to Be Positive

To lock in the takeaway message from this chapter, I would like you both to complete a short exercise. This task will help you clarify specifically where you need to create more positive energy in your marriage. If you take this exercise seriously, you will learn exactly what you need to do to transform your relationship in this area.

First, schedule a time when neither of you has any pressing responsibilities and plenty of time to talk. When you agree on a time, choose a place that is relaxing for both of you such as a place that holds good memories and is safe and comfortable. Make a commitment to meet at that place and time.

Second, when you meet, minimize any distractions. If you have children, find someone to watch them. Other than for an emergency, don't look at your cell phone. Be sure you have a pen and paper to write down the thoughts you share with each other, and make a commitment to listen well to each other and to be honest.

Third, make a list of five specific times that both of you agree were times when you truly enjoyed being together as a couple. What made those times so enjoyable? Could you re-create the environment or situation that led to the joy you felt?

Fourth, discuss how often you experience joy, peace, and contentment in your marriage. Daily? Weekly? Monthly? Or maybe only one to two times each year? Discuss what would need to change for these times to occur more often. Develop a plan for creating space and time in your relationship for these joyful experiences to happen at least every week.

Fifth, make a list of the things that interfere with your relationship being joyful and positive. Look over this chapter again before you discuss the following questions:

Are there negative communication patterns that need to change?

Do you compete with each other rather than cooperate?

Do you criticize each other more than you praise and build each other up?

Finally, identify three specific areas of your relationship that you can choose to change to make your marriage more positive. Once you identify these areas, develop a clear, workable plan for making changes in these areas.

## The Choice to Communicate Positively

When you make the choice to communicate positively in your marriage, you will both benefit from the peace, contentment, and joy you will experience. Instead of competing over scarce resources, you can cooperate as a team. Instead of breaking each other down with criticism, you can build each other up with praise.

If I were a betting man, I would wager a steak dinner that your children, extended family, friends, and coworkers will all notice how much happier you are. Moreover, they will benefit from the choices you make, as the choice to be positive in your marriage will rub off on your other relationships. This choice will truly affect all areas of your life in a profound way.

This choice to be positive is about making life better. There are many times in life when we ruin opportunities for really great experiences by being negative. Take it from someone who has made the wrong choice in this area too many times in his life. Making the choice to be positive can make even the most difficult situations better while making the rest of life sweeter in so many ways.

*five*

# I Choose to Let Go of Old Baggage

We all bring baggage into our marriages. Some of us have baggage from childhood experiences, some from the effects of parents' marriages or relationships, and others from prior romantic relationships. Not all the baggage is damaged, of course, and our past can teach us a great deal. However, some of the baggage creates significant problems in our relationships.

The goal of this chapter is to help you understand the relationship patterns you may have brought into your marriage from your childhood and your previous relationships. Many couples develop patterns of interaction based on their baggage from the past. With knowledge of these patterns, you can learn positive strategies and stop using ineffective ones.

If you understand how you developed these patterns, you can change the ones that are dysfunctional. You don't have to be held hostage by the pain of the past and simply repeat patterns from previous relationships. But for this to happen, you must first understand your past, honestly assess what is happening in your marriage now, and choose to control the future of your marriage. This is not an easy choice to make; it is often easier to act in ways that are familiar and feel safe. I am suggesting that you take the road less traveled, which, as Robert Frost said, "made all the difference."[1]

## Baggage from Your Family of Origin

The family you grew up in has undoubtedly left its mark on you. Whether you adopted your family members' values and modeled your life after them or did everything in your power to become the opposite of all they stood for, they had an effect on you. Some of you barely knew your family of origin, while others of you may be closer to your parents and siblings than you are to your spouse.

Many of you learned about marriage from your parents. Depending on how blended your family was, you may have had several sets of parents as role models. Perhaps you had grandparents, aunts and uncles, or others from whom you learned about marriage. Regardless of who the role models were, we are talking about the examples you were shown of how married partners talk, act, communicate, and manage conflict.

These examples were not all good. Numerous couples have told me they learned how *not* to be married from their parents or other family members. They witnessed yelling and screaming, affairs, alcoholism, and divorce that led them to say, "I am not sure how to act in marriage, but I know I don't want to do *that!*"

I remind couples in premarital counseling that they are not just marrying each other. They are marrying into a family—

parents, siblings, cousins, grandparents, and maybe even a crazy Aunt Lucy and weird Uncle Jim. Marriage is a package deal, and couples need to understand that.

One husband I worked with wanted to support his mom when she made suggestions about raising his first child. His wife, however, was highly offended when he, in her view, "took his mother's side." The allegiances and relationships that existed in the family of origin often create significant conflict in marital relationships.

Terry Hargrave and Franz Pfitzer, in their book *Restoration Therapy*, describe their theory of how family-of-origin experiences shape future marriage relationships.[2] Terry and his wife, Sharon, wrote a small group curriculum titled *Marriage Smart* that they use to help couples understand how these patterns play out in their adult relationships.

In their book, Hargrave and Pfitzer describe their premise that feeling unsafe or unloved in a marriage relationship triggers memories and emotions of previous childhood experiences of a similar nature. Essentially, they believe that these marital reminders of childhood pain create a pain cycle in the relationship. When in this cycle, most partners display one or more of the following four responses:

1. Blame someone else for the pain
2. Blame themselves for the pain
3. Become controlling in response to the pain
4. Try to run away from the pain

The experiences we have as children, especially the painful ones, set the stage for our later relationships. They are powerful influences on the way we interact with our partners, often in unconscious patterns that we are unaware of. Identifying and understanding them can help all of us make different choices in our marriages.

## Baggage from Your Previous Romantic Relationships

Some couples I have worked with were attracted to each other precisely because each of them was *not* what their previous partners had been. Others were repeating the same patterns from one or more past relationships, and they were at risk of making the same mistakes they made in those relationships.

If you were in a relationship with someone who was controlling and dominant, you may have learned to keep your feelings to yourself to avoid conflict. If you were in a relationship with someone who was needy and dependent, you may be wary of getting too close in your current relationship.

When couples have been in previous relationships, they bring all sorts of other baggage with them. Also, there may be children from previous relationships who make constant contact with the "exes" necessary. And even if the divorce was amicable, it can be hard to change expectations from the past.

## → Learning to Let Go of Old Baggage

Everyone wants to know how to overcome old habits. From trying to lose weight to overcoming alcohol and drug addictions, we have been trying to find a solution for decades. I don't claim to know as much about overcoming addictions and old habits as the twelve-step groups, but I do know one thing: learning to change old patterns involves recognizing where we are in the process and getting out of it.

These patterns are long-standing coping methods that you may have used for years. If you have had previous romantic relationships, you likely learned some of these coping strategies there. You may also have learned them from observing your parents.

Letting go of the baggage from previous relationships and your family of origin involves several steps. First, it is important to talk about your family of origin and your previous relationships with your current partner. Whether you are starting a new marriage or have been married for a while, talking about the choices you made in previous relationships is important. I know some of you may want to just move on and forget the past, but if you do that, you might make the same poor choices in your current relationship.

Another important step is to learn what triggers cause you to respond in a certain way. For instance, if a previous partner was obsessed with time and never being late, you may have conflict if your current partner makes a comment about you being late. If a parent often yelled in anger, you may be sensitive to your partner raising their voice.

One other step that might be helpful in letting go of old baggage is for each of you to have a mentor, accountability partner, or therapist with whom you can share your triggers and patterns. A person outside the relationship with whom you can be honest and open can help you work on the things you need to individually address.

Now you are ready to learn what I believe are two of the most helpful skills in this book. The patterns from the past, whether they come from your childhood or previous relationships, were successful and useful when you developed them. These behaviors and patterns helped you cope with the challenges you faced at those times. However, they may no longer be effective if the reasons you used them do not exist in your current marriage. In addition, the longer you are married, the more patterns you develop in your current relationship, and not all of these are constructive or helpful either.

The next two exercises will teach you how to stop a negative, destructive process before it gets worse by understanding where you are in the process and choosing not to continue down that path. These exercises are useful for changing destructive patterns from your childhood, from previous relationships, or from earlier times in your current marriage.

## EXERCISE
## Learning to Take a Time-Out

One of the most effective parenting interventions is the time-out. When a child's behavior gets out of control or parents need to change the direction of a child's behavior, they have the child take a time-out. The same principle that works so well with kids can work wonders for your marital relationship. The goal is to learn how to work together to effectively disengage when your interactions are not healthy.

Any type of choice that leads to negative interactions in your marriage, such as yelling or hurtful comments, can be defined as destructive behavior. The next time you begin to see signs of a negative interaction or an unhealthy pattern of interaction with each other, practice each step in this exercise. Keep track of how quickly you are able to get out of the cycle and how successful you are at interrupting the negative process.

### Step 1: Ask for a Time-Out

Either one of you can call for a time-out, but you both need to commit to honoring the request when it is made. You can't pursue the fight or chase your partner around trying to make them keep talking. When either of you calls for a time-out, you both agree to let go of your desire to win the fight and trust that taking a break is best for both parties.

You should ask for a time-out whenever you realize you are becoming so emotional that you may say things you regret and start down the path toward destructive behavior. You may notice that you are getting too angry or fighting too hard to get your own way, or you may become aware that your partner is too tired or frustrated to think clearly. Simply agreeing to table the fight for the time being is far better than saying or doing hurtful things.

### Step 2: Don't Drop the Issue

The person who asks for the time-out can't just drop the issue and never bring it up again. That leaves the other partner frustrated and upset with no idea when the issue can be addressed. That's not fair. Whichever partner asks for the time-out, whether for their own sake or because they see the fight is getting out of control, you both have to agree on a time when you can talk about the situation again.

The important thing here is not to use the time-out to run away from the conflict. I always recommend that the partner who asks for the time-out should let the other partner know when they think it might be okay to talk about the issue again. Whether you take an hour to calm down or you wait until the next day, you both need to agree on when you will try to talk again.

### Step 3: Consider Not Talking for a Period of Time

I tell every couple I work with that I would rather they choose not to talk about an issue (or even not talk at all) than to say or do harmful things they will regret. Rather than continue down that harmful path toward additional destruction, I suggest they learn to step back and let the issue go until we can talk about it in counseling.

The same goes for you, whether you are a couple who fights repeatedly or very rarely. If it appears that you are going to get into a destructive fight, I would rather you not talk about the issue or simply not talk at all for a while. The important thing is not to create another negative, hurtful experience that you will have to forgive each other for.

If you can't seem to talk about the issue without fighting, consider involving a third party. This could be a professional counselor or psychologist, but it doesn't have to be. A pastor, a close friend, or another third party could serve as a mediator to help you talk through the conflict. The important thing is to choose to take a time-out rather than continue the harmful conflict cycle.

### Step 4: Use a Specific Word or Phrase to Call for a Time-Out

Over the years I have discovered that couples who succeed at using time-outs to prevent conflict escalation develop specific language for calling for a time-out. Choose a word or a phrase that will allow you both to understand the signal and respond immediately.

Some couples have chosen the phrase "I need a time-out." I know . . . original, right? Other couples have chosen phrases such as "I need some space" or "Can we take a break?" Just choose something that will be crystal clear so that you both know this is the signal for stopping the fight, as you have both agreed to do.

I cannot overstate the importance of learning to take these time-outs. You may not get this skill right all the time at first, and that is okay. But you need to make a commitment to each other to practice this skill over and over until you are able to prevent the downward spiral almost every time.

## Getting out of the River before Going over the Falls

Couples have told me over and over that one of the most important things they have learned in marriage counseling is the Niagara Falls analogy that I am going to share with you now. This is extremely effective in understanding how to let go of old baggage as you learn how to stop using the old patterns that no longer work.

With some practice, you should feel more confident that you can stop an unhealthy cycle when it begins and choose to take a time-out. However, to succeed at breaking old patterns, you have to learn to see them coming and make choices early in the process to avoid bad consequences. The problem for many couples is that they wait too long to take a time-out.

I spent many years in the federal prison system. No, I am not a felon—I worked as a psychologist in federal prisons. During my time there, I became acquainted with the work of William Fleeman[3] and a video he created using Niagara Falls as a metaphor for problems such as substance abuse and anger. I started applying his metaphor with the inmates I worked with who had anger problems.

After I left the prison system, I contacted Fleeman's organization to ask if I could build on his thoughts by applying the image of Niagara Falls to marital conflict. They were kind enough to give me formal approval to use it for this purpose. I first wrote about this in *The Controlling Husband*, and what follows is based on that book.[4] The Niagara Falls metaphor is a truly revolutionary way to view where you are in the conflict process and increase the likelihood that you will make good choices early in the process of conflict.

Most of us have seen a waterfall, but Niagara Falls has immense power. The water current is unbelievably strong, and if you are in a barrel heading toward the falls, you have no shot at getting out of the water. You can see the falls coming, and you can swim as hard as you want to get out of the water, but you *are* going over. Here is the thing most people don't know about Niagara Falls. If you head upriver a few miles, the water is calm and peaceful. You can float in the water or swim around. There is absolutely no warning that death and destruction await just a few miles downriver.

As you get closer to the falls, signs warn that danger is approaching. These signs are not hard to see if you know what to look for—you know, the "Danger, Death Ahead" type of sign. If you pay attention to these warning signs, you can do what you need to do to get out of the water.

I believe that most marital conflicts seem to take place at the edge of Niagara Falls. Maybe this happens because of the time or place you are arguing or because of the patterns you have developed over time. Regardless, many of these conflicts take place when there is little chance of a positive outcome.

What if you could see the falls coming in your marriage and get out of the water *before* you went over the edge and ended up in a fight?

The takeaway here is that the closer you get to the falls, the harder it is to get out of the water. The stronger the current (your emotions), the harder it is to make the choice to get out of the water (take a time-out) and the more likely it is you will go over the falls (end up in a fight).

## EXERCISE
## Learning to Avoid the Falls

The first step in learning to avoid the falls is for each of you to make two lists. First, make a list of warning signs that you are not okay and are at risk of going over the falls. Write down anything you feel inside your body or any thoughts or experiences that let you know you are upset, angry, frustrated, or feeling any other type of emotion. You are trying to identify any warning sign that lets you know there is a problem in the relationship or with yourself.

Next, make a list about your partner. Write down what you see in your partner that lets you know they are not okay. Maybe they leave the room or speak louder. Perhaps they become quiet or give a look of intimidation. As with the first list, try to think as far "upriver" as you can.

The next step in learning to avoid the falls is to rank the items in terms of which behaviors/actions/feelings happen closest to the falls. Assign 1, 2, 3, etc. to the warning signs that mean a fight is imminent. Those that are farther upriver might be 4, 5, or 6.

Now you each have two ranked lists of the warning signs for a fight. There are several things you can do with these lists. Some couples I have worked with have printed out a picture of

Niagara Falls and the river above it and written the warning signs where they belong on the river. Others have put the lists on little cards, laminated them, and placed them in their purse or wallet as reminders.

Be creative about how you want to use the lists, but make sure you don't just file them in a box. You need to talk about them and discuss the best ways to be aware of the warning signs and take action when you notice them. These lists will serve as a helpful guide to where you are in the conflict process and help you avoid escalating to a fight by getting out of the river before you go over the falls.

Fair warning—almost every couple I have worked with has found that even when they are armed with the knowledge that the falls are coming up soon, they sometimes make the wrong choice. Many marriage partners, including my wife and I, have looked each other in the eyes, well aware of what was coming, and made this choice: "You want to fight? Okay, let's fight!" Then they plunged right over Niagara Falls into a fight. You will probably do this too, at least once if not more times, and that is okay.

Here is the thing. I am going to ask you not to hold what happens after you go over the falls against each other. If both of you choose not to take a time-out and to go over the falls, it is simply not fair to hold the things that are said or done against each other. You both knew what you were getting into, and it makes no sense to stay angry when you both knew what would happen.

I am not saying you have free rein to be mean and hurtful. If you go over the falls, you still have to get out of the water as soon as you can, try to take a time-out immediately, and minimize the damage. However, holding on to resentment and bitterness about what happens when you go over the falls just makes things worse.

84

## Al and Peggy

The baggage you bring to your marriage often has a huge effect on how you respond to each other. In this next example, a husband and wife (we will call them Al and Peggy for those of you who remember the '80s TV show *Married with Children*) have learned how to parent from their own parents, but the difference in the styles they learned creates conflict in their relationship.

Peggy grew up in a family in which children were, as she put it, "seen and not heard." She and her siblings did what they were told, spoke to adults only when spoken to, and followed rules because they didn't want to make Mom or Dad mad. They kept their feelings to themselves and didn't yell or argue.

Al, in contrast, spent his youth with siblings and parents who put all their feelings out on the table and argued loudly with each other. Nothing was set in stone, and parents and children came up with mutually satisfactory household rules.

Fast-forward to Al and Peggy married with three kids, and you can probably predict what they were arguing about in my office. Peggy wanted their kids (thirteen, nine, and seven) to do what they were told. "Rules are rules," she said. "The kids need to do what they are told to do and quit arguing." Al had a much different view, wanting to allow the kids to voice their concerns and come up with rules they could all live with. Even after thirteen years, this couple was not making parenting choices as a team.

Peggy was extremely frustrated. "I don't know why he is so mad at me. I just want the kids to behave." Peggy chose to get angry at Al for not "backing her up." "He gets to be the good guy, and I'm always the bad parent. It's not fair!" She also chose to discipline the children on her own instead of working with him to decide what they could both agree on.

Al, for his part, felt as if he needed to balance Peggy's toughness. "One of us has to listen to them and hear their side of the story." At times, he made the choice to take their side and support them without even hearing why Peggy had disciplined them. He had grown to believe she was just too tough on the kids and that he needed to offer a softer approach, although he had to admit this often led him to choose to support the kids over his wife.

The work in therapy consisted of talking about their many family-of-origin issues. Both Al and Peggy had to let go of many things they had held on to from their pasts and create space for a new set of family rules and expectations. Peggy learned to discover the value of not being the sole authority and disciplinarian in the house, giving up some of the power that entailed. Al began to consider the value of boundaries and expectations.

Both partners made the decision not to discipline the kids individually but to tell them they would talk to each other first. They also set up a discipline/reward chart that everyone in the family agreed to. They were pleasantly surprised to discover that the kids responded to (and liked) having some clear behavioral expectations that provided structure. They learned that to move forward as a new family, they had to disengage from the models of the past.

## The Choice to Let Go of Old Baggage

Wow. That was a lot of information for one chapter, wasn't it? You learned about the baggage you may have from your family of origin and previous romantic relationships that may have contributed to the patterns you now face in your marriage. You discovered how to use time-outs in your relationship to avoid some of those old patterns from your past, and you learned to see Niagara Falls coming and get out of the river before you go over.

Let's just stop for a moment. This is a good time to take a breath. Maybe you can put the book down for a while, go out to dinner with your partner, and spend some time enjoying how your relationship is changing. Notice the way you both feel. Share the excitement and the fear with each other. There is no one right way to feel about all this, but sharing the experience and listening well to each other are important.

Here is something I know for sure. The choice to let go of old baggage will change your life. Perhaps more importantly, it sets the stage for the next choice we will consider, the choice to forgive. We are going to be talking about repentance and moving forward. These are tough choices to make if you live in the past. Letting go of old baggage allows you to see new choices and new options that you never realized were possible.

Choosing to stop replaying old tapes from your childhood and past relationships will set you free in ways you cannot imagine. I know it is not easy leaving the past behind and moving into an uncertain future. Change is just, well . . . hard, and uncomfortable, and different. But when you make the choice to let go and your vision is not clouded by your past, you can see yourself, your mate, and your future in a completely new light.

*six*

---

# I Choose to Forgive

## Part 1: *Choosing Forgiveness over Unforgiveness*

"I forgive you." Three simple words shouldn't be that hard to say, right? But what exactly do you mean when you say, "I forgive you"? Do you mean "I forgive you, but . . . I won't forget what you did . . . you better not do it again . . . I'm going to resent what you did for a long time"?

Forgiveness is a process that involves much more than just an apology and a response. It involves several elements that are all part of an ongoing process. Before we get to that, though, let's look at what happens when partners choose not to forgive.

### Choosing Unforgiveness

You can choose forgiveness or unforgiveness every time your partner does something that hurts you. Everett Worthington and Nathanial Wade define *unforgiveness* as "a cold emotion involving resentment, bitterness . . . along with the motivated avoidance or motivation against a transgressor."[1] In other words, when you don't forgive, the resulting bitterness and resentment color your relationship for years to come. I understand that you may have good reasons not to forgive your partner. If your partner has repeated a behavior many times after promising not to do it again, you may feel as if they don't really want to change or are incapable of change.

I believe that when you choose unforgiveness, you choose to believe your partner can't change, you choose not to trust them, and you choose to focus on the past instead of the future.

### "I Don't Believe You Can Change"

Some partners really don't believe the other is capable of change. I have heard clients call their partners "relationship challenged," "emotionally retarded," and "totally incapable of change." These statements make me sad when I hear them, as they indicate a complete lack of hope in the future of the relationship.

Where does this negative attitude and hopelessness come from? Most often it stems from the "fool me once" mindset. Clients make statements such as "You can't seriously expect me to believe he can change when it hasn't happened in ten years!" It is interesting to note that these same clients often expect to be given second chances when they struggle with change.

### "I Don't Trust You"

Choosing unforgiveness means that you are actively deciding not to trust your partner. When you have broken someone's trust in the past, didn't you want another chance to prove you could be trustworthy? The double standard we have for expecting trust as opposed to offering trust has always intrigued me.

This double standard has something to do with the vulnerability it takes to trust someone who hurt you. You cannot really forgive someone authentically without allowing yourself to be vulnerable again. This is a risk many of us are hesitant to take.

### "I Forgive You, but I Will Never Forget"

Have you ever said, "I forgive you, but I won't forget what you did"? This statement is a double message: I want to forgive you, but I want to remember how you hurt me. You are placing a set of conditions on any forgiveness you do offer. It is as if you are keeping a scorecard and want to hold on to the power that being ahead in the game provides.

If you hold a grudge, you probably don't believe your partner is sorry for what happened or you are not willing to be vulnerable and trust that it won't happen again. There is something powerful about having your partner "owe you." We hold on to that scorecard tightly, fearful to be vulnerable and give up the power it gives us.

## Physical Effects of Unforgiveness

Choosing not to forgive has a cost, and sometimes the price tag is high. Bitterness and resentment can even have physical consequences. Recent studies have found that holding on to resentment and bitterness can actually make you sick. Concordia University researchers reported findings from a study in which they found that harboring bitterness can affect a person's metabolism, immune system, and even basic functioning of major body organs.[2] Michael Linden wrote about a proposed new mental health disorder in a chapter titled "Posttraumatic Embitterment Disorder—PTED" in a 2011 book on embitterment. This is reported to have long-lasting effects on a person both mentally and physically.[3]

Think about other types of mental health experiences that affect physical health. Long-term anxiety can lead to stress and heart attacks, depression can interfere with healing and recovery, and anger can lead to all sorts of physical harm. It makes sense that bitterness and resentment can lead to physical illness as well.

## Charlene and Rico

Charlene and Rico never thought they would be in a counselor's office. When they first got married, both of them thought the world of each other. They hadn't known each other long before they got engaged and then married, but they were young and in love.

In my office, after two years of marriage, they wondered who they had married. Charlene had become friends with a male coworker, who had gotten the idea she was interested in him. She would later admit in counseling that she liked the attention and did spend some nights working late with him, even having coffee with him after work a few times. When she and Rico had some difficulty communicating, she would talk about her marital problems with this coworker. However, she told him she was married and would never cheat on Rico.

If she had told Rico the truth then, he would have been angry, but it probably would have been something they could have worked through. However, worried that he would get upset, Charlene hid the relationship from Rico. When she rejected the coworker's advances, the man became angry and told everyone in the office they had slept together.

Word of this got back to Rico, and at first, he believed Charlene completely. Then, little by little, details started to come out. First, she said, "Nothing is going on! It's all lies!" Later she admitted that she had spent some late nights at the office with him but insisted, "He's just a coworker. Nothing happened."

When she later admitted she had gone out for coffee with him a few times, Rico stopped trusting her. He began to see her as a liar and wondered what new revelations would come out in the coming weeks. *Maybe she did sleep with him. If she lied about having coffee, she probably lied about that too.* He wondered if she could ever change, and he began to think that maybe he had married someone he couldn't trust.

Charlene apologized over and over again. "I am so sorry. I never meant to hurt you. What can I do to make you trust me again?"

Even after several months in counseling, Rico didn't know what to believe. "I don't know how to trust you. You said you were telling the truth, and you were lying. Why should I believe you now?"

## The Four Elements of Forgiveness

Some people think of forgiveness as a quick process that occurs with very little effort. However, I believe there are four steps that couples need to learn in order to forgive. They are essential elements in the developmental process of forgiveness.

### Apology

The first step in any process of forgiveness is always an apology. There really isn't any movement forward until someone says, "I'm sorry." Think for a minute, though, about the last few times someone said those words to you. Did one apology seem more sincere than another? Not everyone feels that saying those two words is enough.

Our society has even changed the words "I'm sorry" to a glib "My bad." A simple gesture of slapping your own chest to indicate something was your fault seems to suffice. Many of us don't have any other model than the two-step dance of "I'm sorry" and "I forgive you." I don't believe that is actually forgiveness—it is more like an agreement to move on. Maybe that makes sense for two people who bump into each other on the sidewalk, but more is required in a marriage.

An authentic apology involves trying to understand why you offended the other person. It also involves making a real effort to prevent it from happening again. This is a choice you have to make over and over. Rather than a matter of simply saying "I'm sorry," making a sincere apology is an ongoing process that requires commitment and follow-through.

In a marriage, words can cut deeply and actions have consequences. When the person you love lies or betrays you in some way, your feelings don't just disappear because they say, "I'm sorry." Forgiveness takes more than that, which is where repentance comes in.

### Repentance

Let's talk about the words *remorse* and *repentance*. Remorse is usually seen when a partner appears to regret what they did, while repentance adds the implication that there is a resolve to change. When you demonstrate true regret for your words or behavior along with evidence of a desire to work hard to prevent further offense, you will likely be seen by your partner as "sincerely" apologizing.

This is why it is important to do more than simply say you are sorry. You have to convince your partner that you are truly remorseful for your actions and that you have a plan in place that will make it possible for you to prevent a repeat performance in the future. This gives your apology some weight.

Think of it this way. If you don't show remorse for your actions along with a clear desire to create lasting change in yourself, you don't give your partner any reason to believe you won't do the same thing again in the future. In essence, you are saying you feel bad that you hurt your partner but not bad enough to do something to prevent it from happening again.

I would encourage you to offer an apology only when you mean it—when you believe that what you did was wrong and you want to put in the work to prevent doing it again. In my opinion, it is more intellectually honest and relationally healthy not to apologize at all than to apologize when you don't mean it. You may, in fact, do more damage with an insincere, forced apology, as it can cause your partner not to believe future apologies.

### Accountability

The forgiveness process begins with a sincere apology based on true remorse. This is followed by repentance, which is characterized by an awareness of why the offense occurred and hard work to prevent it from happening again. The next element is accountability.

Accountability is important in the forgiveness process because it involves both parties setting some expectations for the future. Suppose Charlene apologized for lying to Rico, but then she kept doing it in the future. Rico's forgiveness shouldn't be conditional on Charlene's behavior, but it is hard to forgive someone again when they keep doing the same thing.

However, accountability involves more than holding each other responsible for making changes. It is also about developing a plan for success that clearly identifies all the factors that contributed to what happened. This includes both partners, as one partner's behavior may influence the ability of the other to make the necessary changes.

Accountability is a two-part process. First, you both need to agree on what circumstances led to the offense, and this may involve choices that both of you made. This is hard for some couples, as the offended party may think their partner is the only one who needs to change. In reality, both partners often made choices that set the stage for the act that occurred.

Second, once you have both agreed on what things need to change for both of you so that the offense won't happen again, you have to hold each other accountable for these changes. To be clear, I am not suggesting that you make a comment every time the offense occurs, as looking at the greater body of work may mean that 95 percent success is an outstanding level of change. However, with some choices, such as an affair or lying, even one failure may be unacceptable.

### Expecting Success

Accepting the apology of your partner means you are convinced that they feel true remorse for what they did and are working hard to prevent it from happening again. Offering forgiveness means you are telling your partner that you plan to treat them as if the offense did not happen. Of course, you don't forget what happened, but you choose not to let it affect your interactions with your partner. This means you make the choice to let go of bitterness and resentment by wiping the slate clean.

I strongly suggest that you do not utter the words "I forgive you" unless you truly mean you are relinquishing the right to hold the act against your partner. Just as I suggested you not apologize unless you are willing to work hard to prevent the offense from happening again, you should not offer forgiveness unless you are honestly willing to let go of resentment and bitterness and treat the person as if the act hadn't happened.

Even if the party who was offended can make the choice to offer authentic forgiveness, that is still not the end of their responsibility. The second choice that partner has to make is to rebuild trust in the relationship by expecting the offending party to succeed in the changes they have committed to make.

The entire process of forgiveness can fall apart without this last piece of the puzzle. If you offer forgiveness but you maintain the expectation that your partner will not succeed in changing their behavior, you run the risk of a self-fulfilling prophecy. Trust and intimacy cannot grow in the shadow of the expectation of failure.

You have to believe that your partner is capable of change and expect that they will succeed in that endeavor. This is much harder to do than you might think. It is much easier to protect yourself by expecting your partner to fail than to open yourself up to future pain by expecting success.

Learning to trust your partner again involves changing assumptions and expectations that are resistant to change. You've been hurt before, and you can live in that "fool me once" state of mind that causes you to expect the worst. Choosing to trust your partner and expect that they will succeed allows the forgiveness process to be completed and both parties to move forward in an intimate, trusting marital relationship.

## Choosing to Forgive

Choosing to forgive involves three specific decisions. To truly forgive, you need to choose to give up the power that resentment and bitterness give you, choose to accept that forgiveness is not fair, and choose to help your partner change.

### Give Up Your Power

Forgiveness involves willingly choosing to give up power, as you can no longer hold the act against the other person. You have to throw out the scorecard and not bring it up in the future.

Your partner may have apologized and taken responsibility for what happened, but what they did really hurt you. For many of us, it feels good to be one up on someone, and we don't want to give up that power. You have to willingly choose to forgive the debt and balance the scales, because as long as the relationship remains unbalanced, there is little room for trust, security, and love.

### Accept That Forgiveness Is Not Fair

Most of us have an intrinsic need for justice. When you have been wronged, you often feel strongly that the person who hurt you needs to pay for what they did. Justice, in the truest sense, would require punishment. However, the "eye for an eye" approach is better described as revenge, and forgiveness does not live in such places.

One of the hardest lessons to learn is that forgiveness involves letting your partner off the hook. You may be thinking, *That's wrong on so many levels! They get to hurt me and get away with it? That's just not fair!* You know what? It's not fair, and it's not supposed to be. Forgiveness is about giving up your need for justice and willingly accepting that you are offering to balance the scales when there is no just reason to do so.

### Help Your Partner Change

If your partner has hurt you, it is difficult to put your pain aside and focus on how you can help them make better choices, but this is a necessary part of choosing to forgive. It may be helpful to let your partner know that you have made mistakes yourself and have truly appreciated those who have forgiven you. In addition, your partner will benefit from your willingness to understand the choices that were made. When you offer to help your spouse make changes, they may begin to feel more comfortable sharing the backstory behind the choices they made. You may even learn to see your part in what happened. As you see their side of the story, you may find it easier to support your partner in making the changes necessary to prevent the problem from occurring in the future.

## Back to Charlene and Rico

Think back to the couple we met earlier in this chapter. Although Charlene's behavior had started the conflict, it became clear in therapy that she had learned from her mistake and was working hard to establish boundaries with coworkers so that a similar situation would not happen in the future. The roadblock to transformation for this couple was Rico. He had been rocked by the fact that she had lied to him, and getting past what had happened was proving difficult.

I suggested to Rico that he think about Charlene's level of trustworthiness in light of what I called her "current body of work." Judging her on the past hadn't worked, so I challenged him to look at her behavior over the past twenty-four hours or over the past week. He began to take notice of her hard work every day to be honest with him, and he saw evidence that she was being honest even when doing so caused her fear.

Both of them needed to make a change. Charlene had to repent and invest significant effort in choosing to behave differently. In return, Rico had to focus on who Charlene was today and not judge her based on her past behavior. Working as a team, they were able to forge a new level of trust. Despite the pain her choices had caused, their relationship was stronger. In their words, the trust and love felt "real" and "authentic," and that was what they both were looking for.

## EXERCISE
### Learning to Feel Empathy

One of the best ways to learn to choose to forgive involves learning to feel empathy for the person who wronged you. When someone hurts you, think about how the choice that person made protected them and served a purpose. When you consider why the person acted the way they did, it is harder to remain resentful.

I have adapted the following exercise called an empathy interview from an excellent workbook by Everett Worthington.[4] This workbook, along with many self-directed and group manuals for promoting forgiveness, is available at no cost as a Word download at www.EvWorthington-forgiveness.com. Take a few minutes right now to complete this exercise. Either one of you can start, as you will reverse roles later in the exercise.

Think of a recent time when your partner did something that was hurtful to you, and your partner apologized and accepted responsibility for it. If you both agree this situation is safe to talk about, use this for an empathy interview. Ask your partner the following questions:

Why did you do what you did?

What made you choose that specific behavior or those specific words?

How did doing what you did solve a problem or meet a need for you?

Did you feel any pressure to do it? If so, what caused the pressure?

Did you think about how I might feel?

Now, as the offended party, tell your partner what you learned about the reasons behind their actions.

When you have finished the first interview, switch roles, choose a new situation in which you were the offender, and complete the same exercise.

Finally, talk about what you learned about having empathy for each other during this exercise. You should both have learned a great deal about being sensitive to your partner's emotions and how to understand your partner's behavior rather than becoming bitter and resentful.

## The Choice to Forgive

Learning to forgive instead of holding on to resentment and bitterness may be one of the healthiest choices you will ever make. This choice will affect much more than just your marriage. When you realize that all marital partners make mistakes at times and you show grace and understanding, you will find that you begin to give everyone in your life more leeway to be human.

You will likely be surprised by the amount of effort it took to maintain all those scorecards about who let you down, when and where it happened, how much it hurt, and so on. When you learn the power of forgiveness, you begin to wonder why you ever worked so hard to be an unforgiving person. After all, what did it ever really get you?

In this chapter, you have worked hard to understand the process of forgiveness and to learn the skills needed to make forgiveness a part of your marriage relationship. However, there are some big things that some of you have to forgive—things such as affairs or other painful betrayals. To help you with these issues, the next chapter focuses on how you can forgive the really "big stuff."

This choice, like all choices, is not one you can avoid. In other words, not making a choice is a choice. You either forgive or you don't; there isn't anything in between. This is one of those choices that will define you as a person. For some of us, our faith teaches that forgiveness is an expectation, while others simply know that holding on to resentment and bitterness destroys relationships. Regardless of your motivation, forgiveness is just a better choice.

*seven*

---

# I Choose to Forgive

*Part 2: Choosing to Forgive the Big Stuff*

In the last chapter, we learned about forgiveness and the benefits it offers compared to the consequences of unforgiveness. The skills you learned will help you choose forgiveness over resentment and bitterness. However, couples have consistently told me that they struggle to forgive things that deeply hurt them, often with a deep sense of betrayal. In this chapter, we will look at how to forgive your partner for the really big stuff.

## Forgiveness after Major Betrayals

To understand the challenges involved in forgiving the big stuff, let's discuss several areas that qualify as major betrayals in marriage. After reviewing some of these, we will meet a couple who had to work through forgiveness after an affair.

### Sex

Affairs are one of the most significant offenses that couples have to forgive. They can be sexual or emotional, although sexual affairs are often harder to forgive. Learning to believe that your wife is "out with the girls" is a difficult mountain to climb when that is what she claimed when she was with another man.

Other sexual issues also create forgiveness issues for couples. Pornography use can create a huge rift between a husband and wife. More often, it is the husband who is getting sexual satisfaction from pornography. This can lead a wife to feel extremely hurt and devalued, believing that he likes looking at pictures of other women more than being with her. In this case, forgiveness can be complicated by the ongoing secrecy and guilt that pornography involves, as well as the effect it has on intimacy and closeness in the relationship.

Couples also often differ in levels of satisfaction with their sex lives. One partner doesn't think they have enough sex, while the other feels they have too much. One partner wants more variety, while the other thinks their partner's desires are "weird." Some couples can't even talk about sex. They just turn off the lights and pretend the problems will go away. Still others stop having sex altogether, a phenomenon known as "the sexless marriage."[1]

Partners can cross the line in work relationships. Some people have a "work wife" or a "work husband" to whom they become so close that both they and others come to view them as a couple. This closeness can lead to inappropriate actions, including sharing intimate details of each other's lives or becoming closer to each other than to their spouses. The risk of an affair becomes quite high when these lines are crossed.

Such betrayal doesn't happen only at work. It can also occur in church, on a sports team, or in any organization. Whenever one partner chooses to get close to someone, often of the opposite sex, that relationship can threaten emotional and sexual intimacy and trust in the marital relationship. Moreover, the forgiveness process is quite complicated in these situations, as the relationship often continues even after the offense has occurred.

One wife explained how sexual betrayal felt by saying, "It's like he stuck a knife in my back when he had that on-line affair. The fact that he thought it was okay to say those intimate things to someone other than me was bad enough. Then I found out he kept doing it and lied about it even after he saw that therapist for sex addiction. That was like he just kept twisting the knife in my back on purpose." This is one example of how much harder the forgiveness process is when the initial betrayal is multiplied by lies and deceit after the fact.

### Money

Financial matters can lead to a great deal of pain as well. I have worked with people who hid unpaid credit card bills or made poor investments and then covered up their actions. Other people have lied about their job situations or income that was or was not being earned. Money just seems to be a strong catalyst for partners to lie to each other.

A husband might be extremely hurt and frustrated when he has to deal with the past financial choices of his wife, while a wife might have to take a second job to pay for poor investments by her husband. Financial choices often create resentment and frustration because of the sacrifices that are required to fix such mistakes. It becomes easy to blame the partner for the end result, even if the choices that were made at the time may not have been that unreasonable or selfish.

### Lies

Many times we don't think of small lies as problems. We even justify them by calling them "little white lies." We don't think they harm our partners and believe we are protecting them. In a marriage relationship, though, a pattern of telling small lies can quickly lead to larger, more dangerous deceit. The problem is that small lies lead to big lies, and big lies are hurtful and destructive to relationships.

Most of the time, brutal honesty is a better choice than even small lies. I am not saying you need to be mean, as you should always be tactful, kind, and empathic when you share your honest opinion. However, when it comes to telling the truth in your marriage, it is always best to be honest with your spouse. Don't fall for the lie that what your partner doesn't know won't hurt them or, even worse, that you are actually protecting them by lying. The problem with lying is that it forms a pattern of deceit that your partner will have difficulty forgiving. Specifically, the problem in the forgiveness process comes when your partner has to believe you are trying to change. Expecting success is hard for your partner when you have demonstrated a pattern of hiding things from them.

### Broken Promises

If you are married to someone who promises to do something and then breaks that promise, you will have difficulty trusting them in the future. As with lying, not being true to your word creates an expectation of distrust. One client told me, "I know he doesn't have my back. I've just come to expect that he won't do what he says he will."

Distrust is multiplied if you develop a pattern of breaking your promises. You are better off admitting you won't or can't do something for your spouse than promising to do it and not coming through.

### Talking behind Your Back

Another behavior that creates feelings of betrayal is saying things to other people behind your partner's back. Whether the words are spoken to a family member or a coworker, they are, at best, disrespectful and hurtful and, at worst, destructive to the relationship. What you say may get back to your partner, and even if it doesn't, talking behind your partner's back is wrong.

You may think that you can talk about your spouse and they will never know. The question is, Why would you cut down your spouse? Maybe you and your buddies make comments about your wives that you think are funny, or perhaps you talk with other wives about the worst qualities of your husbands. In both cases, the activity is hurtful, negative, and disrespectful to a person you claim to love, as well as very difficult to forgive if you get caught.

My wife was once involved in a small group in which the women complained constantly about how their husbands folded the towels. Jan kept thinking, *Why aren't you happy that he is at least folding the towels? Who cares if they aren't perfect?* When you hear yourself criticizing your partner to others, you need to check yourself.

### Selfishness

We will talk more about selfishness in the next chapter, but it is worth mentioning here. When you act in selfish and self-serving ways, such actions can be hard to forgive. Everyone acts selfishly at times; it is the repetition that is hard to forgive. When your partner starts to expect you to think of yourself before them, you have a problem.

The unique problem that selfishness presents is the way it makes a partner feel. It can be painful to feel that you are in a marriage all by yourself. You begin to stop asking your spouse for help, assuming they won't care anyway. Maybe your spouse is focused on work all the time or doesn't care to listen to you. Whatever the reason, you feel as if you don't have a partner.

## Dave and Lisa

Dave and Lisa represent many couples I have worked with who have experienced an affair. By the way, even if you have not experienced an affair in your marriage, you can learn a lot from this couple. Just insert whatever betrayal you have felt from your spouse in place of the affair to make the story real to you.

When we began our work together, Lisa was extremely angry, threatening to get a divorce after telling Dave he had to move out of the house because she wanted a separation. Dave was staying with a friend, and he was missing the kids and Lisa.

Lisa had asked him to leave after she discovered an email on their computer to a woman she did not know. The email made it clear that they were having an affair. He claimed it was just a one-night stand with someone from work. However, as she questioned him, that story fell apart, and it became clear that he had seen her numerous times and had grown quite close to her.

After a few weeks of counseling, Lisa told Dave he could move back into the house, but she was still hypervigilant about his every move. She checked his computer often, expecting to find another email that confirmed he was still seeing her. For most of the first few months we worked together, Lisa had to work hard not to expect that Dave was cheating on her again. Despite his constant professions of love for her and his repeated promises never to cheat again, she was, in her words, "waiting for the other shoe to drop."

To help Lisa believe that Dave could change, we talked about changing her belief that "Dave is a cheater and will always be a cheater." This took some work, as he had hurt her deeply and she felt that she could never look at him the same again. Often, the partner who has been betrayed has the most difficult time moving on, even if the other partner wants to make different choices.

After a few months, Lisa began to build some trust in Dave. He was an avid golfer, but at least two times in the past he had told her he was golfing when he had been with the other woman. It was hard for her to believe him now, but she was making progress. For a few weeks, both of them looked calmer during sessions, and they talked more about the future. It appeared things were moving in the right direction.

Then it happened. Lisa's worst fears were confirmed when she found another email account on their computer. She discovered that Dave had been emailing the woman he had the affair with from another account. The entire time they had been in counseling, Dave had been communicating with the other woman.

Dave tried to tell Lisa that he did not want to be with the woman again but that he was, in his words, "trying to let her down easy and not hurt her by breaking it off completely."

Lisa looked at him and said, "Seriously? You are seriously going to sit there and tell me you are worried about her feelings? What about my feelings? You have got to be kidding me!"

When you were a kid, your parents probably told you, "If you do something wrong, we want you to tell us the truth about what you did. If you lie about what you did, things will be much worse for you." You probably didn't believe them, but most of the time your parents were right—telling the truth would have been better.

In a marriage in which a betrayal has occurred, forgiveness is hard enough when it involves only a specific act or behavior. When you have to forgive your spouse for the lies they told to cover up what they did, it is that much harder. Trust me on this one, folks. Your parents were right. You will have a much bigger mess to clean up if you lie to your partner about what you did. Dave and Lisa were dealing with this level of forgiveness.

I can hear some of you out there saying, "She doesn't have to put up with that. Just leave the guy and get a divorce." Many couples do choose that option. However, they had three kids together, had invested many years in a marriage that had many strengths, and shared a religious faith that put a high value on marriage and commitment.

Lisa had three options:

1. She could get divorced (no one would blame her).
2. She could stay married but fully expect Dave to have another affair (this would lead to bitterness and resentment).
3. She could stay married and choose to forgive Dave for both the affair and the lies.

Lisa canceled the next couple of counseling sessions, saying she had to think things through. About a month later, they made another appointment to see me. When they came in, Lisa was still extremely hurt and angry, but she had decided to give counseling another try. Dave was fairly quiet but not defensive, and he accepted responsibility for his actions and wanted to show Lisa he still loved her.

Over a period of a couple years, we worked through many aspects of what had occurred in their marriage. It became clear that the affair was not the first challenge they had faced, and it was certainly not the only problem in the relationship. Trust issues had existed for a long time, and there had been other issues they had not dealt with that formed the backstory for the affair.

 ## It Takes Two to Forgive

As we learned in the last chapter, forgiveness is a two-way process. It is a complex interaction of one partner apologizing, showing remorse for their actions, and working hard to make sure what happened doesn't happen again. In addition, it involves the other partner offering forgiveness, making the choice to expect success from their partner, and giving up the power that resentment provides.

Let me say this very clearly. Dave was completely responsible for his actions. The partner who commits the offence is always 100 percent responsible for his or her actions. However, there are almost always other factors that contribute to one partner's choice to do something that hurts the other.

At first glance, it would seem there is only one marital partner to blame for an affair. After all, only one of you had sex with someone else. Here is the thing I tell all the couples I work with: no one ever wakes up in the morning and says to themselves, *I think I will have sex with someone other than my spouse today.* That is not how it works.

A series of events, sometimes over years, usually leads up to an affair. A gradual distance develops between you and your spouse. Perhaps resentment builds when one of you works long hours and spends more time with a "work wife" or a "work husband" than your spouse.

Lisa and Dave had a huge breakthrough in their marital work when they realized that there were problems in their marriage long before the affair. They had always thought their relationship was fine. It wasn't until the affair happened that they seriously looked at the state of their marriage. They still had to work through the process of forgiveness for the affair and Dave's lies after the affair, but they began to realize that the affair was far from the only problem they had in their marriage.

Lisa went to great lengths early in our sessions to point out that nothing she had done was as bad as what Dave had done. She repeatedly talked about how no matter what she had done, she hadn't slept with someone else. When clients feel this way, I call it a "hierarchy of sins." One partner defines the other's behavior as worse than their own behavior to minimize their own choices.

What led to long-term change in the marriage was that both Dave and Lisa began to look at the affair as one of many mistakes they had each made. Lisa had kept her feelings to herself for many years, choosing to let things build up rather than dealing with conflict when it occurred. She had also spent a great deal of time with the kids, often talking to them about her feelings more than to her husband. In addition, her career had become quite challenging, and she found it difficult to keep up with all the demands on her time.

For his part, Dave had focused on his job and distanced himself from the family by working long hours. When he formed a close relationship with a female partner at work, he didn't pay attention to the lines he was crossing. He began to talk to her about his marital problems, choosing to talk to his work partner rather than to his wife.

The point here is that both spouses began to realize they had engaged in hurtful, destructive behavior at times in the relationship. Yes, Dave slept with someone else, but over the years each of them had made choices that were selfish. They began to see the affair as one of many bad choices they had made, and as they did so, seeing one partner's behavior as worse than the other's became less important.

113

### → Explanations, Not Excuses

A big part of forgiveness is understanding the difference between an explanation and an excuse. We use these terms interchangeably in our language, but they are quite different. When a couple is dealing with forgiveness, the differences become clear.

An explanation helps both partners understand why something happened and make sense of it. The distance and disconnection between Dave and Lisa would be an example of an explanation. The separation and isolation that had developed prior to the affair help explain why they both met their needs for relationship outside the marriage—Lisa with her children and Dave with his coworker.

In contrast, an excuse is a reason people use to avoid accepting responsibility for their actions. When a partner uses an excuse, they are trying to give a reason why they should not be blamed for what happened. The partner is clearly saying, "This was not my fault. You should not hold it against me."

If Dave were to say, "If you hadn't been so involved with your job, the kids, and your friends, I wouldn't have had an affair," that would be an excuse. He would be trying to blame Lisa for his choice to have an affair. That clearly isn't true, as there was no excuse for his choice to have an affair. He made the decision and was completely responsible for the consequences of his actions.

When you think that your partner is making an excuse, you don't feel much like forgiving them. You don't believe your partner is taking responsibility for what they did. Other times, though, your partner isn't making an excuse but is simply explaining why something happened. If you consider

114

this possibility, you might be able to understand the reasons behind the choices your partner made.

## The Choice to Forgive the Big Stuff

Dave and Lisa used the therapy process to make the choice to stay married. Lisa was able to forgive Dave and expect him to remain faithful in the future, but this was largely because Dave accepted responsibility for his behavior and took clear steps to prevent it from happening again. Their story should give you hope, as it shows that when you put in the work and learn to make different choices, transformation and change are possible. The choice to forgive is an intensely personal one. My own understanding of forgiveness comes directly from my Christian faith. I am honestly not sure I would have the strength to let go of bitterness and resentment without God's help. The choice to forgive, and forgive, and forgive again goes against our desire for justice and fairness.

That is why this choice is so closely tied to the next choice we will discuss: the choice to be unselfish. You have to be willing to give up getting your way if you want to forgive. If you want to make a permanent choice to be forgiving in your relationship, the next two chapters are very relevant. Forgiveness and unselfishness each provide clues to the other, so we now move on to learning how to choose to put the needs of your partner before your own.

*eight*

# I Choose to Be Unselfish

*Part 1: Choosing Unselfishness over Selfishness*

Everywhere you look, people do selfish things. You need look no further than a trip to the grocery store. You want to change lanes, and instead of letting you in, the driver in the other lane speeds up. You get to the store, and as you get ready to turn into an open parking spot, a sports car comes from the other direction and takes the spot you have been waiting for. If you have ever seen the movie *Fried Green Tomatoes*, the Evelyn Couch approach in this situation is to ram the car out of the way and say, "Face it, girls, I'm older and I have more insurance." I would strongly recommend you not take her approach, however.

Once you get inside the grocery store, you wait in line at the meat counter. It's your turn next, but another customer cuts in front and orders ahead of you. Two young high school students push by you in a hurry to get somewhere and don't even apologize for bumping into you. As you check out, you observe a customer yelling at the checkout clerk for ringing something up wrong. You have to wonder what happened to basic human kindness and compassion.

Sometimes selfish acts have more serious consequences than losing a parking spot. A husband knows how much his wife and kids love him, but he makes the decision to have an affair anyway. A coworker wants a promotion, so she spreads horrible lies about her competitor to assure she gets it. Look at the things politicians will say about each other to win elections. The world seems to revolve around mottos such as "It's all about me" and "Look out for number one!"

When this "me first" mentality is brought into a marital relationship, it causes real problems. With the world encouraging both of you to focus on your own needs, sharing scarce resources in a marriage and thinking of your partner before yourself become difficult. Choosing to have a healthy, loving relationship and to focus on meeting each other's needs can be a challenge.

## The Self-Focused Relationship

Some people seem to thrive in a marriage focused on meeting their own needs first. Consider this classic power couple. Jamal had worked his way up to vice president at a powerful investment company, and LaToya was a highly successful real estate agent. Their careers meant everything to them and were a huge part of their identities. However, they had heard their pastor preach on intimacy and connection in relationships, and they came to see me to discuss these issues in their marriage.

117

They had decided not to have children, stating, "Why would we want to have kids? That's great for other people, but it's not what we want out of life." Jamal felt that children "interfered" with success, and LaToya felt there was just no way she had time to be a mother with her real estate career. "It wouldn't be fair to the kids. Children deserve the time and energy they take, but we just don't have space in our lives for that."

To be honest, this couple had to admit that the pace of their lives also left little time for romance and intimacy in their relationship. They had done an outstanding job of becoming first-class business partners, making a great deal of money, buying a beautiful home and expensive cars, and supporting each other's business ventures. But they had little time left over for each other.

As I got to know them, we talked about whether they had any interest in changing the relationship and developing intimacy and closeness. LaToya admitted that she really didn't have a strong desire for intimacy and closeness, and Jamal felt much the same. They had always had a relationship that fit the model of business partners more than romantic partners anyway. They were satisfied that their marriage was meeting their needs, and they decided they had no interest in pursuing a different model of marriage.

I certainly honored their decision not to change their relationship, but it was sad in many ways. If they had considered embracing a new model of marriage that focused on putting each other's needs first, their relationship could have moved to a new level. Focusing on themselves instead of each other prevented them from experiencing the joy and intimacy that could have been possible.

## Lifelong Transformation

To transform selfishness in your marriage, you have to make a careful assessment of your relationship. How are decisions made? Who tends to get their way most often, and does one of you end up sacrificing more often than the other? You need to honestly assess how often each of you acts in selfish ways.

There is a lot more to making the choice to be unselfish in your marriage than you may think. It involves commitment and sacrifice and choosing to focus on your partner's needs instead of your own. Think of it this way. If you are getting your way most of the time, there is a problem, because your spouse is not getting their way very often.

To make a real, lasting change in your relationship in the area of selfishness, you need to do more than just become a better listener or send flowers a few times. This type of change is a heart thing. You have to want to become a different kind of person. I tell the couples I work with that if they want to change their marriage in a truly transformational manner, they have to be prepared to leave the counseling process as completely different people than when they started.

## The Everyday Decision to Be Unselfish

The truth about whether you are acting in selfish or unselfish ways is always seen in the decisions you make. In the end, it doesn't matter how you view yourself in this area. In fact, we are often the worst judges of our own character. What matter are the choices you make regarding your partner, the behaviors you decide to engage in, and the way your choices make your partner feel. You learn who you truly are when you honestly look at the decisions you make every day.

119

Many times truly unselfish acts occur when we make small decisions on a daily basis. John Wooden, the legendary UCLA basketball coach, said, "The true test of a man's character is what he does when no one is watching."[1] How do you treat your spouse when you won't get credit for your actions and you simply have to choose whose needs to meet?

Husbands, think about this for a minute. During your normal day, do you call your wife for no reason, just to see how her day is going and to make her feel cared for? Do you offer to watch the kids so she can go out with her girlfriends? Think about the last time you wanted to watch a ball game or play softball. Did you assume she would watch the kids while you had fun?

Wives, how about you? When you are at work or home, do you stop what you are doing to think about how you could make your husband's day easier? Is he at the bottom of the long list of things you have to do, or does he even appear on the list at all? Ask yourself whether you put as much importance on taking care of him as on taking care of your own needs.

One husband and wife I know wake up each morning thinking of ways to serve each other. Their desire to make life easier each day is contagious, as each act of caring leads to reciprocal kindness, and this affects those around them.

When they talk to each other, they don't interrupt each other. Both partners listen carefully to what the other says before they share additional thoughts, and they genuinely seem interested in the other's opinions. They don't always agree with each other, but when they differ, it is with respect and admiration for the other's alternative point of view.

They usually walk hand in hand, and they look directly into each other's eyes when they are speaking to each other. Having been married for over fifty years, they share a history of inside stories that provide a wealth of connection and intimacy. They do not invest time and energy into conflict and discord, as they know life is short and their time together should be invested wisely. I believe there is wisdom in the choices they have made that we can all learn from.

## EXERCISE
## Learning to Make Decisions

Sometimes the consequences of our choices are bigger than a phone call or flowers. Suppose you have a job opportunity in Boston and your spouse has a promotion offer in Los Angeles. Many situations in marriage just can't be resolved with both partners getting what they want; there are too many times when there are limited resources. What a husband or a wife chooses in these difficult situations says everything about how selfish they are.

This is a simple exercise you can use to examine the way you make decisions in your marriage.

First, as a couple, choose a recent decision you made that you are both comfortable talking about that led one or both of you to become frustrated or angry with each other.

Second, without talking to each other, write down your complete memory of everything that occurred. When did the conflict begin? What did you do? What did you observe your partner do? What thoughts did you have?

Third, compare your notes with each other. What differences are there in your memories? Why might your memories be different? What do you both now believe might be the "truth" about the incident you have been discussing?

Fourth, discuss how a final decision was made. Was it a compromise? Did one person get their way? Were you both satisfied with the decision? Did you focus on your own needs or your partner's needs?

Fifth, talk about the usual way you make decisions as a couple. Does one person get their way more often? Does the person who makes the best argument "win"? Do you alternate who gets their way each time?

Finally, talk about the changes you would like to make in how you make decisions. Think about what you have learned, and choose the best, healthiest process to follow moving forward in making decisions.

The goal of this exercise is to help you understand how you make decisions, change parts of the decision-making process that aren't working, and gain insights into how you can focus on each other in the future.

## Selfishness at Work in a Marriage

In my work with couples, selfishness is almost always an issue in one way or another. Whether it drives how decisions are made, creates distance between partners, or causes conflict, selfishness is a significant factor in the health of a marriage. In contrast, unselfishness can be just as strong a factor in creating a healthy, intimate relationship.

Let's look more closely at how this plays out. Consider Michael and Jessica, who have been married just over a year.

They are starting to move out of the honeymoon phase, getting to know each other more deeply and seeing some of each other's faults. I often work with newly married couples whom I have seen for premarital counseling. One of the biggest adjustments in the first year of marriage is that both spouses realize the other isn't perfect and that they must learn to accept each other's faults.

Michael had been on his own for a while, so he hadn't had to follow anyone else's rules. He had gotten used to thinking of his own needs first, as he made decisions on his own and spent most of his time by himself. Couples are getting married later in life now, so more frequently, I see people who have had a lengthy time on their own and are used to doing what they want.

Jessica grew up as a fairly typical Millennial kid, with parents who focused more on being her friend than holding her to behavioral standards. Her parents had gotten her out of some consequences in high school when she had made a few bad choices. She grew up fairly entitled, as evidenced by her belief that since she had graduated from college, the world owed her a good job with excellent benefits.

Neither Michael nor Jessica were severely narcissistic, excessively vain, or conceited. One of the biggest myths about selfishness is that someone who is selfish is a self-absorbed egomaniac. Jessica and Michael were not egomaniacs, but they both had a level of selfishness born out of their childhood and adult experiences that created a strong desire to get their own needs met.

When they were single, this wasn't a problem for Michael or Jessica. They could focus on their own goals and needs without anyone objecting, other than the occasional friend or family member who was frustrated by their self-focus. When they got married, however, the need for more sacrifice and unselfishness became clear.

Jessica and Michael started to realize that their relationship was becoming quite competitive, as they found themselves fighting for their individual needs. They needed another way, and they began to consider what unselfishness could look like in their relationship. For this to happen, they realized they had to learn what sacrifice was all about.

This turned out to be a significant task in therapy. Jessica had to confront her own entitlement, and Michael had to deal with his strong need for independence. Change was slow but steady, and eventually they chose a marriage based more on sacrifice than selfishness.

### → Sacrifice

The concept of sacrifice gets a bad rap in today's world. People often look at sacrificing as losing the game or giving up and quitting. Making the choice to sacrifice for your partner doesn't mean you are "losing." In fact, it may be the key to winning in your relationship.

Scott Stanley has studied sacrifice for much of his career. He and his colleagues have discovered that sacrifice is an integral part of commitment and strength in relationships. People tend to be more willing to sacrifice if they see the relationship lasting and have a clear identity as a couple (for instance, as husband and wife). Specifically, they found that sacrifice in a marriage is a predictor of the success of the marriage.[2]

A famous quotation attributed to Henry David Thoreau goes like this: "Sacrificing your happiness for the happiness of the one you love is by far the truest type of love."[3] Hmm . . . what do you think about that? I know you had a reaction, positive or negative, when you read that.

On the one hand, giving of yourself to make your partner happy sounds like the unselfish thing to do, and that is what this chapter is all about. In fact, in the next chapter, I will even make the argument that focusing on your partner instead of yourself may be the best model of marriage we have.

On the other hand, something about the suggestion to "sacrifice your happiness" rubs us the wrong way. I am not sure I like the way the Thoreau quotation sets up the equation. Why does one partner have to give up happiness for the other to be happy? Can't both parties be happy in a loving relationship? In fact, there are times when you can actually find *more* happiness in sacrificing for your partner, and I will talk more about that in the next chapter.

Sacrifice is often seen as a zero sum game in which one partner's gains equal the other's losses. That is not how marriage works. Marriage is more like the gestalt concept that the whole is greater than the sum of its parts. Working as a team, offering compromise and sacrifice to each other, and working toward the best solution to a problem can result in greater happiness and satisfaction for both husband and wife.

## Commitment

In addition to your willingness to sacrifice, your level of commitment to your partner is central to the choice to be unselfish. Psychologists at UCLA agree with Scott Stanley that commitment and sacrifice are closely tied. They studied 170 couples over eleven years and found that the couples who were willing to make sacrifices were significantly more likely to have long-lasting and happy marriages.[4]

Researchers at the University of Denver looked at two very different kinds of commitment.[5] The first is called "constraint commitment." It involves feeling as if you have to stay in the relationship because leaving would be difficult. This type of commitment feels more like being stuck or imprisoned in a relationship, and it is not healthy.

The second type of commitment I can really get behind. This type is called "personal dedication commitment," and it occurs when four things happen: (1) the partners view themselves as a team, (2) they have a long-term view of the marriage, (3) the marriage is a priority, and (4) they make sacrifices for each other or for the good of the marriage.

According to the first element, you have to view yourselves as a team. Sometimes the needs of the marriage, or your partner, may be greater than your own individual desires. Remember Spock's immortal wisdom from *Star Trek II: The Wrath of Khan*? He was talking to Captain Kirk as he was dying and said, "The needs of the many outweigh . . . ," and Kirk continued, "the needs of the few." As he died, Spock concluded, "or the one."

The other three elements these authors discuss are also vital to making unselfish choices in your relationship. Thinking about your relationship as a long-term commitment allows you to make good long-term choices for the benefit of the marriage rather than focusing on short-term gains. Making your marriage a high priority means that the choices you make will be based on what's best for both of you rather than just you. When you make sacrifices for each other, or for the good of the relationship, you are choosing to be unselfish.

"It's all about me" becomes "It's all about us." This is the premise on which the model of marriage presented in the next chapter is based.

## The Choice to Be Unselfish

We make hundreds of decisions to be unselfish every week. Some don't require too much effort: holding the door for someone, waiting for the other driver to go when you both got to the stop sign at the same time, letting an elderly person go before you in the fast-food line. Others take more effort.

Choosing to be unselfish means choosing sacrifice and compromise and commitment. These are not easy choices. In our self-centered world, it is easy to think of ourselves before our partners. To make the choice to be unselfish, you have to be willing to put your own needs to the side and make your partner's wants, needs, and desires your primary goal.

I believe the key to making this choice in your marriage is identifying your model of marriage. Don't worry—if you don't know what your model of marriage is (or even what that means), the next chapter will help you understand the concept and clarify what principles your marriage is based on. It will also help you decide if you want to make the choice to adapt or change your model to one that is more effective and healthy.

*nine*

# I Choose to Be Unselfish

*Part 2: Choosing the "Us" Model of Marriage*

Everyone seems to fit somewhere on the continuum of selfish to unselfish, and this can be seen in the choices they make. Suppose you wake up on a Saturday morning and remember that this is the day a friend of yours is moving into a new apartment. The selfish part of you says, "Stay in bed! You know other people are going to help." The unselfish part of you says, "My friend will get the work done faster if I go, and my friend has helped me before."

I once watched an episode of one of the *Candid Camera* type shows in which an actor portrayed a man at a bar flirting with a woman. The two "victims" of the show (who were not in on the setup) were sitting at a table and watched him blatantly flirt with the woman. Then they watched a third actor (playing the man's wife) walk in. As is usually the case in these shows, some people walked right up and confronted him on his behavior, while others said nothing and didn't want to get involved. Were the people who took action "better" people or just less focused on their own interests and needs?

## Where Do You Fall on the Selfishness Scale?

While I was writing this book, a good friend of mine passed away after a difficult battle with a brain tumor. He was one of those guys who always encouraged others, always remained positive, and almost always chose to place the needs of others ahead of his own. He seemed to naturally think of others first, and people who had known him his entire life said he had always been that way.

My wife is cut from that same cloth. In fact, she thinks of others first so much that she has to remember to let people know what she wants or needs. She asks others how they are doing before talking about herself, gives up what she wants so others can have what they want, and tries to make others happy before herself.

In contrast to my friend and my wife, I have to admit that I have often been on the opposite end of the continuum. I often start with selfish desires and have to work hard to fight against the tendency to be selfish. We don't seem to be born with the same degree of selfishness. For some people, thinking of others first seems to be in their DNA.

So where do you fall on the selfishness scale? I have created a short screening questionnaire to help you take a snapshot of where your priorities currently lie. This is not a formal test; it is simply a screening measure. Be honest as you answer the questions so that you will get a true representation of your relationship. Complete this quiz separately from your partner and answer the questions based on your relationship with your current partner.

### EXERCISE
## The Selfishness Quiz

Please label the following statements T (true) or F (false).

1. _____ I am usually more concerned with wanting my partner to hear what I have to say than listening to what they say.

2. _____ I am more concerned with how my partner feels than whether we resolve a disagreement.

3. _____ I don't care whether I get my way in a disagreement with my partner.

4. _____ During a normal day, I make more negative comments than positive comments to my partner.

5. _____ Winning an argument is important to me.

6. _____ My partner usually brings up the topic of conversation when we talk.

7. _____ During an average conversation, I interrupt my partner at least once.

8. _____ On average, I compliment my partner more than I criticize.

9. _____ Resolving an issue is more important than how my partner is feeling.

10. _____ I am more concerned with making the best decision for us as a couple than with meeting my own needs.

## Selfishness Quiz Answer Key

| | | | |
|---|---|---|---|
| 1. T = 1 | 4. T = 1 | 7. T = 1 | 10. F = 1 |
| 2. F = 1 | 5. T = 1 | 8. F = 1 | |
| 3. F = 1 | 6. F = 1 | 9. T = 1 | |

## Interpreting the Selfishness Quiz

8–10   You usually focus more on yourself than on your partner.

5–7   You often focus more on yourself than on your partner.

3–4   You sometimes focus more on yourself than on your partner.

0–2   You usually focus more on your partner than on yourself.

### Both of You Scored High on Selfishness

If both of you scored high on this quiz, it is likely that you both tend to put yourselves first in your marriage. Don't feel bad. This type of marriage is common today. However, this does create some challenges for you as a couple. For instance, when you both want something, you may have difficulty figuring out how to make a decision. Compromise may be hard for you to achieve. The good news is that if you are both self-focused, you are both likely to voice your opinions. The bad news is that both of you may be likely to want to "win" the battle and have difficulty listening well to what your partner needs.

To improve communication, first consider alternating time during conversations, with one partner speaking for five minutes and then trading off. For couples with two strong-willed personalities, trying to "win the argument" is a critical mistake. Avoiding competition and focusing on cooperation will make it easier to agree to disagree.

Second, since both of you have probably tried to prove your point in the past, you need a new goal for discussions. I suggest you change your goal from proving your point to understanding your partner's point. Focus on learning what your partner wants, since you already know what you want.

Finally, separate the decision from the discussion. Listen to both points of view first and clarify differences you may have. Take time to understand what you each desire as an outcome before you start talking about making a decision. Once you are clear on how you each feel, then consider a compromise that may get each of you enough of what you want to satisfy you both.

### One of You Scored High; One Scored Low

If one of you scored high and one scored low on the selfishness quiz, you likely have a difference in power in the relationship. The partner who scored high may have more control, and the other partner may feel "less than" in some important ways. One of you probably has a stronger voice, and the other may feel unheard at times. Without strong boundaries, the less powerful partner can give up trying to be heard at all.

To improve communication, allow the less selfish, quieter person to state her or his view first so that both voices are heard. I realize this may take you out of your comfort zone, but here is why this matters. If you are the more selfish partner, your voice is almost guaranteed to be heard. You have to ask yourself if you truly want your partner to feel valued and heard as well. If so, letting your partner speak first significantly increases the likelihood this will happen.

Second, the partner who is more selfish needs to repeat what the less selfish partner said. I literally want you to repeat out loud, to the best of your ability, exactly what you heard your partner say. That way your partner can say, "Yes, that's it" or "No, this is what I am saying." This activity is important because it provides validation and clarity that you are both on the same page.

Finally, the more powerful and more selfish partner now has the opportunity to share their views. This is not a time to argue with the other person or "win" the argument. Simply share your views as your partner did. The goal is to be sure both of you feel respected and heard.

### Both of You Scored Low

If you both scored low on the quiz, you may be generally altruistic people in most aspects of your lives. You have probably learned to consider others and naturally think of others before yourselves. This is a good thing and can be very beneficial to a relationship. However, if both of you tend to listen more to the other than share your own views, you may have difficulty making decisions and voicing your opinions. You may sometimes let life happen around you and not be proactive in your relationship, assuming that everything is fine and you don't need to talk about things very much.

To improve communication, first celebrate the desire each of you has to care for and listen to the other. Be thankful that your partner wants to take care of you and hear your concerns. This can't be overemphasized, as this is an important and valuable part of a healthy, teamwork-based marriage.

Second, hold each other accountable for not avoiding conflict. Agree to identify a conflict when it exists and to both share your feelings. Making a commitment to deal with issues when they come up will prevent you from avoiding and burying important issues.

Finally, don't expect that you have to resolve a conflict the first time you discuss it. That might be too threatening or maybe even overwhelming. Just agree that you both want to voice your opinions and clarify your feelings, and then work on some solutions at another time.

## What Is Your Model of Marriage?

For years, I have asked couples, "What is your model of marriage?" Some people give an answer based on their religious faith, stating that their faith gives them a model to follow. Others talk about couples they respect who have been married a long time or books they have read about marriage. Still other couples say they learned the answer to the question from their parents or grandparents.

However, by far the majority of the couples look at me with the classic "deer in the headlights" look and respond by saying, "What are you talking about?" They have never considered this question, nor have they developed a set of expectations and commitments based on the answer to the question.

The question focuses on the choices that lead you to behave the way you do in your relationship and what your goals of being married are. The question boils down to what principles your marriage is based on. Who are you as a couple? What do you stand for? When you can define the core characteristics of your relationship, you can begin to understand what model of marriage you have chosen to follow.

There is no need to worry if you can't answer that question right now. However, by the time you are finished working through the chapters and exercises in this book, it is very important that you clearly identify your model of marriage as a couple. You both need to take this task seriously and think carefully about it, as the key to transforming your marriage lies in identifying and committing to the bedrock principles on which it is based.

## Is Your Marriage a Contract or a Covenant?

Gary Chapman describes the characteristics that define a contract and a covenant. A contract is made for a limited period of time, deals with specific actions, is based on an "if-then" mentality, is initiated by someone who wants to get something out of it, and is sometimes unspoken and implicit.[1] A contractual marriage is a relationship based on each party meeting their own needs and having an "out clause" if it doesn't work out.

In contrast, Chapman says that a covenant is initiated for the benefit of the other person, makes unconditional promises, is based on steadfast love, views commitments as permanent, and requires confrontation and forgiveness.[2] As opposed to a contractual relationship, a covenantal marriage is other-focused and unselfish in nature.

To be honest, I think most engaged couples are too naive and uninformed about their own relationship and models of marriage in general to make a truly covenantal commitment. They say the words in their marriage vows, but they learn what they mean during the early years of marriage. Even with the best of intentions, "you don't know what you don't know."

However, as your relationship grows, the covenant model may be more possible and effective. A relationship based on promises that are kept in order to honor principles that are clearly understood can last a lifetime. It will require making

135

the ten choices described in this book, but the covenantal marriage is unashamedly devoted to a lifetime of making these choices.

It is vital for couples to define the core concepts on which they want their relationship to be based. These things will help them identify priorities in the relationship, define approaches to conflict resolution, and help guide their decision making as a couple. The following exercise will help you identify these core concepts in your marriage.

Look back at your marriage vows. Despite how young and immature you may have been, you probably identified some of these core concepts in the words you said to your betrothed on your wedding day. However, do you actually apply them in your day-to-day married life? Have you kept those promises?

## EXERCISE
## Defining Your Model of Marriage

This exercise will help you understand the principles that are currently guiding your marital relationship.

First, individually create a list of the strengths in your relationship. Identify as many positive characteristics of your marriage as possible. Once your individual lists are done, compare your lists. Decide together on what the top five strengths in your relationship are, and choose a word that best describes each strength.

Second, individually create a list of the challenges that you face in your relationship. Once your individual lists are done, compare your lists. Decide together on the top five challenges in your relationship. Next, think together about what overcoming each challenge would look like and choose a word that describes the characteristic you would like to transform that part of your relationship into.

Third, based on the first two steps, you should have the information you need to create a set of principles that will form your model of marriage. You have a set of five words that describe current strengths in your relationship and a set of five words that describe what transforming current challenges would look like. Together, these provide areas of strength and goals to work toward. These ten words will form the foundation of your model of marriage. Keep this list handy as you will need it for an exercise in the final chapter of this book.

## Two Popular Models of Marriage: The "Me" Marriage and the "Us" Marriage

I believe there are two common models of marriage in the world today. One focuses on what your partner can do for you in the marital relationship, while the other focuses on what you can do for your partner. Think of it like John F. Kennedy's famous line "Ask not what your country can do for you. Ask what you can do for your country." To paraphrase: Ask not what you can do for yourself. Ask what you can do for your partner.

I call these two models the "me" marriage and the "us" marriage. The "me" marriage model suggests that the primary purpose of a marriage is to get your needs met by your partner, with the understanding that if they no longer meet your needs, you can find a new partner who can and will. In this model, compatibility and a good match are extremely important. To see evidence of the popularity of this model, one need only look at the millions of people who utilize online dating services such as Match.com and eHarmony to find someone who will meet their unique needs.

A 2010 column by *New York Times* columnist Tara Parker-Pope was titled "The Happy Marriage Is the 'Me' Marriage." Parker-Pope said, "In modern relationships, people are looking for a partnership, and they want partners who make their lives more interesting."[3]

Elizabeth Thomas expanded on Parker-Pope's claims by stating, "I would like to add my views on Ms. Parker-Pope's piece. The letters M and E at the beginning and the end of the word 'marriage' spell the word 'me.'" She also said, "Without the 'me' in marriage, there is no foundation on which to build a relationship. The more fulfilled we are as individuals, the more fulfilled our marriage will be."[4]

Do we really want marriages that are based on a "foundation of me"? I agree that we are all looking for interesting partners, but I am not sure healthy marriages are founded on each partner meeting their individual needs. In fact, this self-focus may be a recipe for marital discord rather than success.

The real danger in the "me" marriage is that it can lead to rampant selfishness, significant power and control issues, and strong competition for scarce resources. Tim and Joy Downs, in their book *The Seven Conflicts*, noted, "The argument may begin about finances, or personal records, or the way you spend your time, but it ultimately reduces to one of two underlying issues: the desire for Structure or the desire for Control."[5] Tim Keller, in *The Meaning of Marriage*, said, "Self-centeredness is a havoc-wreaking problem in many marriages, and it is the ever present enemy of *every* marriage."[6]

In stark contrast to this approach, the "us" marriage model is about serving your partner and meeting their needs before your own. Servanthood and sacrifice are the watchwords in this type of marriage, with each partner trying to understand what the other partner wants and needs and working hard to provide that.

The "us" marriage focuses on many of the principles in this book. Concepts such as selflessness, praise, forgiveness, and letting go of the past are central to this model. Partners making this choice work hard to cooperate with each other and to develop mutually beneficial interactions. Choosing the "us" marriage leaves both partners feeling honored, loved, and respected.

## Millennials and the "Me" Generation

The Millennial generation, despite being highly committed to social justice issues, also scores extremely high on measures of self-interest and narcissism. This self-focus has resulted in Millennials being dubbed the "me" generation. They were brought up by "helicopter" parents who hovered over them to protect them and often related to them more as friends than as parents.

Craig Blomberg and Elizabeth Sbanotto, in *Effective Generational Ministry*, explained that the Millennial generation's self-focus may be due to having grown up with parents who were hyperfocused on meeting their children's needs and solved many of their problems for them. They feel this generation has a need for immediate gratification as well.[7] These traits lead to a self-focused approach to the marriage relationship. Suppose your entire life growing up was "all about you" because your parents always sheltered you. It's likely that your marriage might need to be "all about you" too.

So we have a "me" generation that is being offered a "me" marriage concept. That combination makes it likely that more and more marriages will be based on people meeting their own needs rather than meeting each other's needs.

## Understanding the "Us" Marriage

It seems that a marriage based on devotion to meeting your partner's needs before your own would have a higher likelihood of success. Think about the issues that couples cite as cause for divorce today: sexual affairs, lack of communication, growing apart, incompatibility. Aren't these all the result of focusing on your own needs rather than on your partner's needs?

The "us" marriage involves making choices that place your spouse's needs before your own. You are completely flipping the script in this approach. Instead of fighting for your own needs, you are fighting for your spouse's needs and your partner is fighting for yours. Instead of trying to convince your partner to give you what you want, you are working to resolve conflicts so that your partner can get what he or she needs.

In my practice, I have seen couples make the choice to switch to the "us" model of marriage with truly transformational results. Time and again, couples who have spent most of their relationship defending their own needs, expectations, and desires are amazed by how much better life is when they work together as teammates. I am not suggesting you give up on everything you want in your marriage. In fact, most couples tell me that this approach leads to them being more satisfied in their relationship than they ever dreamed they could be.

## But What about Me?

Putting your partner first may be a whole new ball game for you, and it may be scary. What happens if you really try to be a giver and your partner doesn't return the favor? There is no question that the "us" marriage is all about trust. You have to believe that your partner will have your back.

Taking care of your partner does not mean sacrificing all your own desires. You have every right to voice your wishes and let your partner know what you want and need. But rather than trying to force your partner to give you what you want by winning a fight, you can each try to meet the other's needs instead.

To be honest, making this choice may be as much about trusting your partner as it is about being unselfish. Later, we will spend an entire chapter on trust, and I hope that chapter will help with the challenges that trust presents in this area. For now, the important thing is not to let your fear of trusting your partner prevent you from trying to become less selfish in your marriage.

## The Choice for the "Us" Marriage

Over the twenty-five years I have been working with couples, one constant has been the destruction that selfishness causes in a marriage. When one or both partners are focused on their own needs, they may win the battle at times, but intimacy

141

and connection in the marriage become collateral damage. The degree of selfishness present is central to almost every decision couples make. It affects how they treat each other on a daily basis, and it sets the priorities for their relationship.

If you didn't have a model of marriage to guide your choices in your relationship, this chapter has presented a model that you can choose to follow if you wish. If you did have a model that you have been using, this chapter hopefully helped you assess how well it is working and determine if some changes are needed. In either case, I believe I have presented clear evidence for the value of the "us" model of marriage and made the case that it can be extremely effective for today's couples.

The reason I believe choosing this model of marriage will work for you is that it simply works better than any other model. This model is consistent with Christian principles, so for those of you who are looking for a relationship based on biblical principles, this model meets your needs. If you are simply looking for a relationship that allows both partners to trust each other, work as a team, and have each other's back, this model works for you as well. It is better than anything else out there right now.

*ten*

# I Choose to Challenge "Unspoken Truths"

Some of the most insidious and destructive elements of a marriage are the assumptions spouses make about each other. Assumptions are sometimes based on previous experiences that have been interpreted and at other times are based on minimal factual information. They are beliefs that have been adopted that later become a part of the reality of the relationship. By the way, this is not a problem only in relationships that are struggling; spouses who are doing well in other areas can be just as guilty of making assumptions about each other.

## "Unspoken Truths"

The problem with assumptions is that they become what I call "unspoken truths." These are assumptions, which may or may not be true, that are accepted as truth in a marriage. Once accepted, partners give up trying to change these beliefs. When a statement such as "He would rather spend time playing video games than doing things with me" becomes a given in a relationship, the reality is hard to change. The assumptions are based on real experience, and partners use those experiences to project the future.

These "unspoken truths" form the basis for how spouses act toward each other and drive much of what happens in the relationship. Once spouses begin to accept these beliefs as givens in the relationship, they become the building blocks for their understanding of each other.

I have heard a wide variety of these statements over the years, and some of them have been quite harsh.

He won't ever change—that's just who he is.

She changed when we had kids; they have always been more important than me.

He cares more about his work than he does about me.

She listens to her mother more than she does to me.

He is just lazy.

No matter what I do, she'll never really love me.

I don't care what he says. I know my husband, and he will always be a cheater.

She tries hard, but she's just not that smart.

Once a loser, always a loser.

I know she had a rough childhood, so it's not her fault if she gives up on us.

He says he works all those hours for us, but I think it's really to prove something to himself.

I think he likes the idea of marriage but just not the reality of being married to me.

Once these beliefs become accepted as fact, they grow strong roots in our minds. They may start out as worries or fears based largely in fantasy, or they may be based on hurtful actions or statements that actually happened. In either case, they become absolutes that serve as filters for information that might prove them to be untrue, and we selectively pay attention to facts and details that support them.

To illustrate how this process works, I want to introduce you to Luke and Laura (whose names are a reference to an old soap opera some of you may remember). This story represents a compilation of the "unspoken truths" I have encountered in my work as a therapist. As you read their story, you will notice the assumptions that Luke and Laura have made about each other; in other words, these are their "unspoken truths."

## Luke and Laura

Luke had always been good at almost everything he did. He was smart, attractive, and athletic. You know the type, right? He was a star athlete in high school and college, was at the top of his class, and dated the cheerleader . . . and yes, Laura had been a cheerleader in high school. She was beautiful, smart, and independent, and when they decided to get married after dating through college, everyone said they made the perfect couple.

Luke and Laura got married just as Luke was starting medical school and working long hours. Laura was a teacher and loved working with kids. Early in her career, her teaching kept her busy, but she still noticed how much Luke was gone.

145

*Laura's unspoken truth*: He might care more about work than me, but I'm probably overreacting.

She also had questions about his free time. How does he find time to play basketball with his buddies when he says he is too busy to go out on a date with me?

*Laura's unspoken truth*: He cares more about his friends than me.

If she ever brought this up, Luke would talk about how stressful work was and how he needed to let off steam. He always had a good explanation, and she usually let it go.

*Luke's unspoken truth*: She doesn't understand how hard I work. I just need some place to let off steam. I am beginning to think Laura is pretty needy sometimes.

When they came to see me, they had been married for almost ten years, and they had two young children (ages five and eight). Luke's practice was fairly well established, and Laura had been working for the city schools for several years, balancing being a young mother and having a career. They went to church on Sundays, Luke played in a local basketball league, Laura was on several committees at the church and helped with the PTA at her school, and they had many couples with whom they socialized.

From the outside looking in, they looked like the model of a successful marriage. If you were to ask members of the congregation at church, they would have said their marriage was awesome. Their pastor knew things were bad, as he had referred them to me, but both Luke and Laura admitted that their friends and family had no idea how difficult their relationship was.

> *Luke and Laura's unspoken truth*: We can't let anyone know that we are struggling. We have to put on a good face for everyone.

When I saw them, resentment and bitterness had begun to set in. Laura needed Luke to be with her on Thursday evenings, but Luke wanted to play basketball to relieve the stress of his job. If he played basketball, she resented that he wasn't with her, but if he spent the evening with her, he resented that.

> *Laura's unspoken truth*: He cares more about basketball than me.
> *Luke's unspoken truth*: She is too clingy. She doesn't want me to have fun.

Their relationship problems were compounded by the pressure they had allowed to become "their life." The pressures of finances, jobs, children, and social expectations were overwhelming.

> *Luke and Laura's unspoken truth*: We have to do everything. Our life is running us, and we have no control over what we do.

Before you get too judgmental and think their problems should be easy to solve, stop and think about your life for a minute. Is it really that easy? You both go to your jobs and work hard all day or night (some of you don't even have the same work schedules). If you work the day shift, you pick up the kids from day care, come home, get them fed, give them the attention they demand (and deserve), and get them ready for bed. It's probably 8:00 or 9:00 p.m. by now. When exactly do you have time for the wonderful "date night" that we therapist types seem to recommend so often?

To be honest, Luke was operating at almost maximum capacity. He was seeing a full load of patients every week, trying to stay in shape with exercise and eating well, and working hard to find some time most days to see his kids, even though he was tired after work. In one session, he said, "I just don't have much energy left for Laura. I know that's not right, but it's true." From his standpoint, if he had to sacrifice something, it would have to be time with her, as cutting back on work, not staying in shape, and not seeing the kids were simply not options.

> *Luke's unspoken truth*: If I have to give up time with her to handle work and my other responsibilities, Laura should understand.

Luke was not a bad guy. He wasn't an egotistical jerk who cared only about himself. He was actually like many husbands out there who still maintain the belief that they can do it all—succeed at work, be a good dad and husband, fulfill church and community responsibilities, work out and stay in shape, and not sacrifice anything. For most people I work with, this is simply not possible. Something has to be sacrificed, as there are finite resources of time and energy.

Now let me be clear. There are husbands who can be jerks. There are men who take advantage of their wives, become jealous and controlling, and even become abusive and violent. I wrote about the devastating and destructive power of control issues in marriage in my first book. I will be the first to say that power and control issues can tear a couple apart.

But this was not Luke. He was just so focused on trying to establish his career, which he told himself he was doing for his family, that he lost focus. He was trying to do everything—meet all the expectations of his work, his family, and his church—but it couldn't be done without some sacrifice somewhere.

*Luke's unspoken truth*: I am doing all this for my family. Laura should understand that.

What about Laura? She was trying to be Supermom by working a full-time job, taking care of the kids and the house, and being a part of her community and church. The phrase we've all heard before is "You *can* have it all!"

*Laura's unspoken truth*: I can do it all—work, kids, marriage, church. I can handle it!

As the years went by, it became more and more clear that this was simply not true. Laura had to make choices, and not everyone placing demands on her could have everything they wanted. Laura had passed up some of the promotions and honors she could have received at work, choosing to miss important meetings so that she could take the kids to ballet or karate lessons.

*Laura's unspoken truth*: I gave up opportunities in my career for our family. Luke should do the same. I don't think he puts our family first like I do.

As a therapist, I have had to learn how to see both sides of the story and try to understand and make sense of both partners' perceptions. I could see how Luke felt trapped under the pressure of the career he had chosen, and I could feel Laura's pain at how distant she felt Luke had become. The chasm between them had become quite vast, and they both felt alone and helpless to change the situation.

After several sessions, it became clear that there were significant differences in the model of marriage they were using. Luke thought his role as a husband was to "become successful, provide for the family, and take care of Laura and the kids." He asked, "What does she have to complain about? I work seventy hours a week for her and the kids, and then she says I'm not home enough. What on earth does she want from me?"

*Luke's unspoken truth*: I'm doing my absolute best here, but it is never enough for her. No matter what I do, I can't please her.

He described being a doctor with "unselfish" language, but I sensed there were more selfish reasons behind his career choices. He believed he had to work long hours to satisfy his partners and build his reputation. It seemed that his occupation had begun to define him as a person and that proving his worth as a doctor was making it difficult for him to find time for his family. He believed his primary role was to earn a great living and provide for his family, but I kept thinking, *At what cost?*

> *Luke's unspoken truth*: I have to prove myself to my colleagues and create a reputation for myself as a physician.

Laura's model of marriage, in contrast to Luke's, was based on the belief that she was supposed to take care of her family and put their needs before her own. If she wanted to do something but one of the kids needed to go to a dance rehearsal or a soccer practice, she almost always put off what she wanted to do. She thought, *As long as the family is happy, that is what matters most, right?*

> *Laura's unspoken truth*: I have to sacrifice for my family. That is my job.

If Luke got upset over something, she attributed it to the fact that he had so much on his plate and was working so hard, and she let it go. Sure, he seemed to overreact at times and could be pretty critical. But how could she complain about that when he had just worked twelve hours at the clinic and visited three patients in the hospital after that? Whenever she did get up the courage to mention something, he would say, "But you knew what you were signing up for when you married a doctor, didn't you?" She couldn't argue with that.

> *Laura's unspoken truth*: No matter what the cost to the family, his desire to be a doctor trumps anything I or the kids might need.

I have developed an exercise that will help you discover the "unspoken truths" that exist in your marriage. For this to work, you have to make a commitment to each other to be honest and transparent in your communication during this exercise. Trying to hide the beliefs you have or protect your partner from feeling hurt by what you believe will not help you identify and change these beliefs.

Fair warning—this is a difficult exercise. The sentence stems are negative, and they are meant to be. I certainly believe we don't say nearly enough positive things to our partners, and I address praising each other in other chapters. This exercise is meant to help you identify the "unspoken truths" you have not been able to voice about each other. This exercise takes a great deal of courage to complete, as these assumptions have remained buried for a reason.

### EXERCISE
### Determining Your "Unspoken Truths"

Complete the following sentences on your own without talking to each other. Be as honest and as accurate as possible.

I wish my partner would be able to _____

_____

_____ .

My partner does not understand that I need _____

_____

_____

_____ .

If I could change one part of myself for my partner, it would be _____

_____ .

My partner doesn't understand that they keep hurting me by _____

_____

_____ .

The biggest problem my partner causes me is _____

_____

_____ .

I wish I was able to understand _____

_____

_____ about my partner.

My partner values _____

_____ more than me.

My partner would not understand that I need _____

_____

_____ .

Something I have never told my partner about our relationship is that _____

_____

_____ .

I wish my partner knew how much _____

_____ from the past affects me in our relationship.

Once you have both completed the statements individually, schedule time to sit down together to discuss your answers. Start with the first statement and trade off sharing your responses with each other. For each question, discuss the following:

Is each "unspoken truth" actually true?

How did each "unspoken truth" develop?

How have these beliefs been maintained?

For any statement you both believe to be true, identify what steps need to occur to change this situation and develop a plan for implementing this change.

For any statements you both believe to be false, identify what steps need to occur for you to stop believing this false assumption and develop a plan for implementing this change.

## Back to Luke and Laura

Luke and Laura were not as helpless to change their marriage as they thought they were. They were more responsible for their situation than they understood and much more capable of changing it than they realized. This is true for many married couples and is likely true for you as well. Understanding that you have control over your relationship is the first step in transforming it.

You should know this about me: I am not exactly the softest therapist in the world. I have a reputation for being straight with clients and being honest about the consequences of the choices they are making. I believe that when people invest the amount of money and time that counseling involves, they deserve an honest, professional opinion.

So with Luke and Laura, I didn't pull any punches. I shared with them that, in my opinion, they had created the situation in which they found themselves and that they could change it if they wanted to. I asked them to consider whether changing their model of marriage to one in which they thought of their partner first might transform their relationship.

The primary change I suggested to Luke and Laura was that they focus on understanding how to meet the other's needs rather than prioritizing their own needs. Initially, they were somewhat confused by this request.

Laura responded by saying, "Are you kidding me? All I do is try to meet his needs. I have put him before myself our entire marriage. Look where that's gotten us!"

Luke, for his part, was pretty resistant to the idea as well. "Dr. Welch, I am not a selfish guy. I'm working my tail off seventy hours a week to provide for my family and take care of everything they need. How can you say I'm putting my own needs first?"

After some pretty direct confrontation, Luke began to admit that he wasn't working hard just to provide for his family. In fact, he was making more than enough money. Much of what he was doing was to further his career and reputation. Sure, being a doctor required a lot of time, but he was averaging about eleven to twelve hours a day and was on call many weekends.

I asked Luke to reassess his choices by asking him what he was spending the money on and how much he actually needed. I also asked him to closely examine how much his partners in the practice demanded that level of effort, as opposed to his own desire to prove his worth to them.

I asked Laura to consider her actions. She felt she was "doing her duty" by sacrificing for Luke, but she now resented doing it more than she felt good about it. I pushed her a bit on this point, asking her if she was really giving in to his needs for altruistic reasons or because she liked playing the martyr. I also asked her to consider whether she had stopped believing life could be any different.

## Change You Can Believe In

The transformational work Luke and Laura did focused on changing the "unspoken truths" they had come to believe about each other. We spent time determining where these beliefs had come from, why they had become truth in their marriage, whether or not the beliefs were valid, and how they could be changed.

Luke and Laura began to make significant progress over the next few months in counseling. We talked about how Luke's belief that he had to prove himself by working long hours came from the work ethic he had learned from his father. He honestly believed the best thing he could do for his family was to provide the best life he could. We talked about how he had made the image of being a successful doctor an idol in his life for which he was sacrificing his family. He had not realized he was sacrificing his relationships with the very people to whom he was trying to show love.

Luke realized that he had come to believe many "unspoken truths." He believed that he had to prove himself to his colleagues, that he was incapable of pleasing Laura, that she could not understand him, and that he was working solely for the benefit of his family. He began to see that when he talked with Laura and told her about his motivations and emotions, she could understand him better. He also realized that his belief that nothing he did was ever enough for her was a complete falsehood.

And what about proving himself to his colleagues? A breakthrough occurred when Luke shared what was going on in his marriage and family with his partners in the practice. To his great surprise, he found that they were willing to work with him and adjust his hours. In fact, some of his partners were having the same issues with their spouses! His choice to share his concerns with his partners led the entire practice to reexamine how they managed their workload and what a good work-life balance looked like.

We spent time talking about how Laura had come to believe that sacrifice and servanthood were the expectations of a good wife. Laura learned that if she never set boundaries and did not let Luke know what her needs were, there was no way he could work to help her get her needs met. She began to realize that she did not have to give up every time they had a difference of opinion. She discovered that when she used her voice and shared with Luke, he was amazingly supportive and willing to compromise.

I recommended that Laura read *Boundaries* by Henry Cloud and John Townsend.[1] These authors do an excellent job of defining what things you should and can take personal responsibility for and those that you need to hold others accountable for. Laura began to understand that she had never set boundaries in her marriage and that when she enforced boundaries consistently, Luke responded quite well.

Laura had become convinced that Luke cared about work and his friends more than he loved her. She came to realize that although there was evidence that he prioritized work over family, this didn't necessarily mean he didn't love his family. She had just assumed that since he spent so much time being a doctor and doing things with friends, he must like those things more. As we made progress in therapy, she began to realize that Luke didn't know how to communicate that he loved her in a language she could understand. His truth was that he was showing her love by providing a future for the family, while her truth was that he didn't care about her as much as he cared about his work. Neither of these assumptions was accurate.

Laura realized that it wasn't the hours Luke worked, but the time away from him that hurt her most. In addition, when he did come home, he was often so tired that he couldn't focus on their relationship or be present with her in any authentic way. We worked on carving out specific afternoon and evening times when they could focus on quality time together, and they started sharing one special time each weekend when the kids didn't interrupt them.

These changes didn't go well at first. Both of them kept letting outside forces interfere with the new choices they were trying to make. However, day by day and week by week, they began making the small decisions to prioritize each other over themselves. The more they made these choices, the easier they became. Eventually, the choices became so much a part of their relationship that they could hardly remember how or why they had ever made different choices.

## The Choice to Challenge "Unspoken Truths"

You can find hope in the transformation that occurred for Luke and Laura. As Luke began to realize how he had prioritized his career over Laura, and as she began to make her voice heard and set boundaries with Luke, their relationship grew stronger and deeper. The choice to become aware of the "unspoken truths" in their marriage, honestly address these issues, and then make different choices, created lasting transformation in their relationship.

The same can be true for you in your marriage. If you will use what you learned in this chapter to identify the assumptions in your relationship and honestly share these "unspoken truths" with each other, you can make a clear choice to live your life together differently. Bringing these assumptions into the light will create a level of authenticity in your relationship that will make it much easier for you to handle the intimacy issues addressed in the next chapter.

Luke and Laura discovered that they had allowed their entire marriage to be based on assumptions and beliefs, most of which they discovered were not true at all. When they made the brave choice to challenge these "unspoken truths" and no longer believe them, their relationship changed drastically. Just like Luke and Laura, you can make this choice to step out of the darkness and into the light. It may be overwhelming at first, but eventually this choice will lead to healing and truth.

*eleven*

# I Choose to Be Intimate

Intimacy. We hear that word a lot these days.

Not satisfied with your sexual relationship with your spouse? You need intimacy.

Worried that your spouse doesn't understand you or listen to you? You need intimacy.

Married to someone who is too busy with their job to spend time with you? You need intimacy.

But what on earth *is* this "intimacy" everyone keeps talking about? When you look up the definition of the word *intimacy*, you find "the state of being intimate."[1] Yeah, like that helps. So you look for a definition of the word *intimate*, and you find that the adjective version of the word has several meanings. It can mean "marked by very close association, contact, or familiarity."[2] Do any of us really believe that just being in close contact with someone makes you "intimate"? If that were the case, we would be intimate with every coworker or neighbor, and we all know that is not true. It can also mean "marked by a warm friendship developing through long association."[3] This seems a little closer to the mark, but it still misses. Just because a relationship has lasted for years doesn't mean you are really close to a person.

## Being Known

Probably the most relevant definition for our purposes here is "intrinsic, essential; belonging to or characterizing one's deepest nature."[4] However, this still doesn't really capture the essence of what intimacy is, in my opinion. Often, when people refer to being intimate, what they are really talking about is being *known*.

Paul Rosenblatt and Elizabeth Wieling wrote an entire book, *Knowing and Not Knowing in Intimate Relationships*, on this topic. They believe that the concept of being known has been ignored by many writers and researchers in the area of intimacy. They have chosen to define intimacy in a way that best suits our current discussion.

Rosenblatt and Wieling describe intimacy as the desire and motivation to know each other and to be vulnerable enough to share yourself with each other. Intimacy includes investing time in learning how each other works, developing relationship rules, and having accountability, safety, and devotion to knowing and being known.[5]

Let me break this definition down a bit. Being known by someone is a process that is both inherently scary and joyous. The level of exposure and vulnerability is extremely high, as you may find that your partner honestly doesn't like parts (or all) of what you share with them. At the same time, if they

161

accept and honor what you share, and even highly value it, then being truly known by someone else is an exhilarating experience.

What these authors are saying is that the intimacy everyone seems to crave so much these days is not just about sex, although that is a part of it; it is not just about communication, although that too is a part of it. Intimacy is, at its core, about letting your spouse past your defenses and protective walls to a place where they truly see who you are.

## Intimacy Is a Two-Way Street

Marriage is a back and forth, give and take enterprise. It is always a teamwork-based endeavor in which you have to work together to succeed. Intimacy is no different. Both of you have to take the risk to be vulnerable and share who you are, and both of you have to learn to accept and love the aspects of each of you that make you, well, *you.*

Imagine what can happen if one of you takes this risk but the other does not. Suppose Vicky bares her soul to her husband, Frank, and he responds positively and supports and accepts her. Vicky continues to share who she is and what matters to her, but although Frank is loving and supportive, he doesn't share anything of himself in return. At some point, if this is not a mutual process, Vicky will begin to resent Frank's lack of participation. She may even stop sharing, feeling that she is on an island by herself.

I usually see couples test the waters in the area of intimacy by sharing a little of themselves, seeing how the other partner reacts, and then waiting to see if they will both take the risk of sharing their inner selves. It is an interactive process, with each partner stepping into the water, checking to see if the other is also stepping in, and then walking out farther into the water if they sense they are both all in.

As with any risky venture, the consequences of one partner letting the other down by not joining them in the process, not accepting what is shared, or outright rejecting the other can be catastrophic. If you let down your walls and let your partner see who you are, and they reject you, it can be devastating.

This is why the choice to be intimate in your marriage needs to be a mutual choice. You need to spend a good deal of time talking about what this might look like in your relationship. Both of you need to be on the same page concerning commitment, expectations, and accountability when it comes to intimacy.

This next exercise will help you begin a conversation about how you can cultivate intimacy in your marriage. The goal is for you to develop a plan for what intimacy can look like in your relationship and identify steps to get there.

## EXERCISE
### Building Intimacy in Your Marriage

Choosing to be intimate is clearly about knowing each other in an authentic way. This exercise provides specific steps you can take to get to know each other in a more intimate and genuine way. You can take your time with each of these steps, as there is no time line for completing them, but the steps work best if you do them in order.

163

### Step 1: Perform Simple Acts of Kindness

One of the most basic things you can do to build intimacy in your relationship is to be kind to each other. Performing simple acts of kindness sets the stage for the next steps in this process. For this initial step, focus on the next two weeks. Over these fourteen days, pick one specific act of kindness every day that you can do for each other. Make a commitment to doing something that your partner will notice and appreciate. These acts don't have to be grand romantic gestures. You probably already know some of the things that your spouse values, so use that knowledge to engage in a specific act of kindness each day.

After the two weeks are over, sit down and talk about how you both felt giving and receiving these simple acts of kindness. Talk about how these acts led you both to feel closer and more appreciated.

If you find that you are having difficulty completing this daily task, ask yourself why that might be. Why is it sometimes so difficult to motivate yourself to say and do things that make your spouse feel loved? If you can figure out what prevents you from doing these things, you have a much better chance of making them happen.

### Step 2: Use a Positive, Encouraging Attitude

This step involves developing and maintaining an attitude of positive encouragement with each other. To start this process, each of you needs to take some time to consider your attitude toward your spouse on a daily basis. Are you negative, grouchy, irritated, or frustrated with your partner on some days? If you have a bad day at work, do you treat your partner with less compassion and kindness? Think about how your partner would describe you if they were being interviewed about the attitude you have on most days.

After you have honestly considered the attitude you present to your partner, sit down together and share your impressions of how you treat each other. Talk about why you sometimes take out your bad mood on your partner. Brainstorm some ways you can work together to encourage each other rather than bring each other down.

Make a commitment to being honest with each other. Tell your partner if you had a bad day at the office. Ask for your partner's support and understanding and give them permission to hold you accountable if you take out your bad mood on them in some way. Making the choice to have a positive, encouraging attitude with each other will do wonders for intimacy in your marriage.

The attitude you present to your partner affects every interaction you have with them from the time you get up until you go to bed. You can ruin entire days or even weeks with a negative attitude. The wrong attitude can cause a significant conflict in the relationship and bring you close to going over the falls. Whether it is your tone of voice, your behavior, or your words, a positive attitude can make all the difference in your marriage.

### Step 3: Use Touch

One of the most intimate things in a marriage is touch. I am not just talking about making love, although that is a part of it. I am talking about all forms of touch: holding hands, hugs, a touch on the shoulder. Touch between a husband and a wife is truly a part of knowing and being known.

This part of the exercise is pretty straightforward. I want you both to make the choice to touch each other more than you do now. Some of you have not touched each other much at all, outside of sex, in years. For those of you who do touch each other regularly, find new ways to use touch to express intimacy in the relationship. Hold hands when you walk down the street

165

or reach over the table and hold hands during dinner. Put your arm around each other or spend intentional time sharing hugs. Walk up behind your spouse when she or he is cooking dinner and give your partner a hug. Kiss each other like you really mean it when you say hello or goodbye.

The word *passion* has great relevance to intimacy. Think about how you kissed each other when you were first dating. Think about the anticipation and intensity you felt when making love early in your marriage. We will talk more about your sexual relationship in just a moment. For now, imagine how much better intimacy in your marriage would be if you touched each other, held each other, and kissed each other with the passion and intensity you felt when you were just married.

Public displays of affection seem to be frowned on, and we have even abbreviated the concept to the acronym PDA as if it were some sort of disease. If you kiss your spouse passionately, you are likely to have someone respond by saying, "Get a room." There are good reasons why some of you don't show public displays of affection, including past negative experiences, the presence of children, and so on. However, if displaying affection in public doesn't create negative consequences and is appropriate, I think that showing your love by kissing, holding hands, and touching appropriately can be a very positive experience.

### Step 4: Talk about Sex

I think we can all agree that sex is very much a part of intimacy in a marriage. The connection between intimacy and sex may explain why so many couples struggle with their sexual relationship. Some couples deal with unfaithfulness, some struggle with pornography and its effects, some have vastly different levels of sexual interest, and some have simply stopped having sex altogether.

166

A big part of this issue is the difficulty couples have talking about their sexual relationship. Rather than being honest when one partner feels unfulfilled, the couple is often too embarrassed to talk about the issue or they pretend it's not a big deal. Some partners settle for a less than great sex life just to avoid talking about the issue.

If you look at the types of sexual challenges couples encounter, almost all of them involve problems with intimacy.

A husband chooses to look at pornography, and his wife feels devalued and unwanted. There's a problem with intimacy.

A wife feels unloved and uncared for and turns to another man to feel attractive and loved. There's a problem with intimacy.

A husband and a wife have sexual issues for so long that they just stop sleeping together. There's a problem with intimacy.

During my years in clinical practice, I have come to realize that most sexual problems couples describe to me are not about sex. They are usually problems with intimacy that are based in communication, relationship, or conflict issues. The sexual relationship is just the place where these problems are most noticeable.

There are certainly times when physical and hormonal problems occur and there is great value in seeking medical evaluation for these issues. In addition, sexual issues can be related to traumatic experiences, and these often require professional psychological assistance.

Much of the time, though, sexual issues are secondary to some of the factors I just mentioned. If you are not being kind to each other, not displaying a positive attitude, and not touching each other outside of sex, these issues can have a significant effect on your sexual interactions.

If you are not happy with your relationship sexually, talk to each other. Honestly assess how passionate, kind, loving, trusting, open, and intimate you are being with each other in the rest of your relationship. You may find the answers to your sexual concerns there.

### Step 5: Share Inside Stories

The personal and private stories of a relationship are one of the marks of a truly intimate marriage. There are so many memories that you and your partner share, especially if you have been married a long time. Some of these are sweet, cherished memories, while others make you laugh until you cry. Still other memories are of challenges and struggles that may be difficult to recall but that make you who you are as a couple.

Many of these memories are so personal that no one else knows them. You know the kind . . . the ones that get remembered when one of you says something and you give each other a knowing look that only the two of you understand. These are special, sacred connections that bond you together as one.

This step of the exercise is not complicated, but just because something is simple doesn't mean it is easy. For this step, you need to schedule a dinner out where you can talk with each other. During this date night, share as many of the special stories of your life together so far that you can think of. It may be a night of laughter, a night of thankfulness, or even a night with some tears. Your goal is to remember the stories that make your marriage unique and special and to draw closer to each other in the process.

It is in sharing these personal, private stories with each other that you see the level of intimacy in your relationship. When you share these stories and experiences with each other, you truly feel known and understood by your partner—they "get you." This level of intimacy takes time and dedication, and it is often experienced most thoroughly by those who have been married a long time.

## John and Amy

John didn't have any intention of getting in a fight with Amy when he came home from work. In fact, he was actually looking forward to seeing her. He hadn't made the sales he had hoped to make that day, but there was nothing he could do about that until the next day, so he was looking forward to getting away from the office. He walked into the house, kissed their four-year-old daughter, Jasmine, who ran to meet him at the door, and went upstairs to change his clothes before dinner.

He came back downstairs and called out to Amy, but she didn't answer. He asked Jasmine, who had returned to playing with her dolls in the front room, "Where's Mommy?"

"I don't know."

John called out to Amy again. "I'm downstairs," he heard her say quietly, barely loud enough for him to hear. John went down to the basement and found Amy doing a load of laundry.

Amy looked up from the laundry with tear-filled eyes and asked, "Do you still love me?" We all know that almost nothing good ever follows that question.

John braced himself and said, "Of course I love you, sweetheart. What's wrong?"

Amy looked at him and said, "You sure don't act like it."

John asked again, "Amy, what's wrong?"

She threw down the laundry basket, stomped up the stairs, and said, "You should know . . ." John followed her upstairs and into the office. When she pointed at the computer, he realized why she was crying. Amy looked at him with a mixture of anger and sadness and said, "You promised you would stop looking at those websites! You promised!"

169

John looked down at the floor in shame and meekly said, "I messed up. I'm sorry."

He wanted to say so much more. He wanted to tell her that he really didn't even feel much sexual pleasure anymore when he looked at the pictures, that he hated himself for what he did, and that he knew how degraded she felt when she believed that the images on the computer turned him on more than she did. He wanted to say how much he wished their sexual relationship was better and that they could, just once, talk about sex instead of just doing it. He wanted to say all that, but he couldn't bring himself to say anything.

This was the scene John and Amy described when they showed up in my office a few days later, desperate for help because they couldn't stop fighting. As with most couples I work with, this fight was less about the act of sex or sexual desires than it was about the fact that they had never learned to talk about sex.

We spent the better part of the next few months unraveling the lies they had told themselves about sex and the assumptions they each had made about what the other wanted. These were lies that had roots all the way back to their childhoods and their adolescent development. Beyond all this, they had also chosen to hide their true feelings and desires from each other, and they needed to choose to love each other with honesty, commitment, fidelity, and respect.

Change began to occur when they identified what the real problems were and what different choices they could make. John had to admit that he had become addicted to getting sexual satisfaction from looking at images on the computer, and he had to make the choice to start attending treatment groups where he could get the help he needed. Amy had to admit that she had taken their sexual relationship for granted and devoted time and energy to almost everything else other than romance and sex in their marriage. They also had to choose to talk about sex and tell each other what they wanted and how they felt.

As they made these changes, they began to realize how connected all these choices were. The more John chose to avoid pornography, the more interest he had in Amy and the more valued she felt. The more Amy chose to show interest in intimacy and physical touching, the more John felt attracted to her. They found that by making specific choices to prioritize intimacy in their relationship, they were able to significantly improve their sex life and, in so doing, greatly improve the quality of their marriage.

## The Choice to Be Intimate

The great thing about intimacy is that it builds on itself. The more you know your partner on a deep level and are known in return, the greater your connection becomes. Even if things have been rocky in the past, there will be many opportunities in the future to build connection and intimacy in your marriage.

The strategies you learned in this chapter for creating intimacy in your marriage truly aren't rocket science. Start by performing simple acts of kindness and cultivating a positive, encouraging attitude in your interactions. Make the effort to touch each other more and be physically close on a regular basis. Learn to talk about your sexual relationship, and share openly about the strengths and weaknesses in that area.

Perhaps most importantly, the choice to be intimate requires creating space and time for your relationship. Inside stories and unique experiences require time away from others and opportunities for creating memories. These experiences are really the true mark of an intimate marriage. You will need to make a commitment to spend quality time together doing the things you both love. If you make this choice, you will learn that these special, intimate times with the person you are sharing life with will far outweigh any of the other priorities that seem so important on any given day.

*twelve*

---

# I Choose Not to Take You for Granted

Why do we sometimes treat the people we love the most in the worst ways? Many of us say things to our spouses we would never say to a stranger in line at the grocery store. We wouldn't have treated our partners this way when we were first dating, as we were too concerned about impressing them.

Think back over the history of your relationship, whether it involves many years or only a few. When did it become okay to stop being polite and courteous? When did even basic courtesies, such as saying please and thank you or cleaning up after yourself, stop happening? Okay, some days are better than others, but somewhere along the line, many spouses end up treating others better than they treat their partners.

## Taking Your Partner for Granted

I believe we often treat others better than our spouses because we take our partners for granted. When the relationship is brand new, you are trying to earn each other's trust and love. During the engagement, there are many reasons to focus on each other, and this continues through the wedding and the honeymoon.

However, sometime in the first few years (or sometimes months) of marriage, you start taking each other for granted. It starts slowly, in ways that are almost too small to notice. Your husband stops getting your coat or opening the door for you like he did when you went on dates, but you tell yourself you don't need a man to do that anyway. Your wife stops coming to watch you play softball like she used to, but you assume she is just busy.

Maybe you have a child or two, and there are always demands on both of you. With work, household chores, and the kids, there is less and less time for each other. Maybe you have difficulty finding time to be alone together, and you start making love less often. You both notice what is happening, but you are just so busy and tired that you dismiss it and begin to almost expect it.

Over a period of time, you even start changing the tone of voice you use with each other. What used to be a kind request becomes a harsh reprimand. "Sweetheart, could you please do the dishes from last night? I would really appreciate it" becomes "Seriously, you didn't do the dishes from last night again?!" Phone calls that used to make you feel connected are replaced by text messages sent in a rush.

Perhaps the worst part of all this is that it is a mutual process in which we often give back what we receive. The more one of you becomes short and hurtful in your comments and tone, the more the other responds in kind. This can quickly spiral out of control.

John Gottman says that it is a short trip from criticism to the much more destructive experiences of contempt, defensiveness, and stonewalling. In *The Seven Principles for Making Marriage Work*, he describes how each of these experiences builds on the last to destroy communication between partners. What starts out as a critical comment quickly becomes a feeling of contempt, resulting in defensiveness from the other partner. It isn't long before a wall is built between the two partners that can be extremely difficult to bring down.[1]

## What Does Taking Your Partner for Granted Really Mean?

Taking your partner for granted clearly indicates that you don't appreciate your spouse fully and don't give them the credit they deserve. It involves being indifferent to or unaware of the value that person has in your life.

Part of the problem is the familiarity that being married creates. You are around each other every day and become complacent. When you were first dating and married, you noticed so many surprising things about each other. Everything was brand new, and you were paying close attention to every detail. As the years go by, the "new and exciting" is replaced by the "old and expected."

Think of it like this. When you come home every day, you park in your garage, open the door into your house, and walk in. Do you ever pay close attention to the door you open? Of course not. You don't stop to notice the way the handle and hinges work together to let you in the house. You just expect them to work.

175

There must have been a time, long ago when you were young, when you were amazed by the miracle of a door opening. We have all seen young children open and close a door, entranced by what they experience as a magical process. After years of opening and closing doors, you no longer see it as magical. In fact, you don't even notice it at all.

Then one day, after many years, the door won't open. You turn the handle and nothing happens, and you can't get into your house. Now you notice the door. When the door breaks, you pay attention to it and all at once you no longer take it for granted. Only then do you think about the maintenance you could have done on the door to keep it in good working order.

You see the connection to your marriage, don't you? Your partner has been right there by your side for years, helping you out in so many ways. At first, you noticed all the things they did for you to make your life easier, but when those things happened year after year, you just stopped noticing.

The tragedy is that many couples don't pay attention to their marriage until it is broken. It often takes a major event, such as an affair or some other crisis, for them to realize the marriage is in trouble. So many things had been taken for granted that it took a critical event to shock the couple into remembering how much they mean to each other. If this chapter is effective, you will learn to pay attention to your marriage and give your spouse the attention they deserve now, before you take them for granted and the marriage breaks.

## Alice and Chris

Alice and Chris had been married for almost thirty years. They had raised three kids together, and they had a pretty

176

traditional marriage. Chris had worked long hours as a contractor his entire life, and although Alice had worked parttime once the kids were in school, she had borne the primary responsibility for raising their children.

They were empty nesters now, as all the kids were out of the house with their own families or in college. They had never been to a marriage counselor before, but they decided they needed to see someone when they realized they were experiencing significant conflict with each other. After I had seen them a couple of times, Chris came in one session with a clear agenda.

"I just know I'm not happy," Chris began. "It doesn't feel like she really cares about me the way she did. She used to do lots of things to make life easier. She would cook dinner for me all the time, and now we end up going out to eat most nights. For many years, she would bring me a cold drink during a football game or stop by to see me at the job site. She just doesn't do any of that anymore. It's like she just doesn't care."

Alice had been patiently listening, with what appeared to be a slight smile on her face. I asked her what she was thinking. She quietly said, "Yes, I used to do all those things."

I asked her if there was a reason she had stopped, and she looked at Chris.

"Chris, during all those years, how many times did you say thank you for what I did?"

Chris looked surprised. "What do you mean? You know I liked you doing all that."

Alice asked, "How would I know you appreciated what I did? You almost never said thank you. It was more like you expected me to do it."

"You know I love you, Alice. I worked my tail off every day for years to provide for you and the kids. I did all that for you."

"That's not the point!" Alice said, becoming more animated. "I got tired of you taking me for granted. I love you too, and I know you love me. It's just that if you keep doing things for someone and they never show you any appreciation, after a while you lose the motivation to do them."

"You really believe I take you for granted?"

"It sure feels that way. I can't read your mind, Chris."

After they stopped talking, I let them sit in silence for a while. Alice began to be a bit tearful, and Chris didn't know what to say. I asked them if they could describe how they were feeling. Chris looked embarrassed when he said, "I thought she knew. I feel like an idiot. I just didn't realize."

Alice, still tearful, said, "I just want him to say it out loud. Sometimes you need to hear it, you know?"

When a couple has love and the desire to work things out, counseling doesn't always need to take a long time. During the next few months, Chris learned how to tell Alice how much he appreciated her and the things she did for him. Alice worked on being more willing to tell him when she felt unappreciated. They made great progress on their goals, as they truly loved each other and wanted the other to be happy and feel loved.

What they did have to do was change some lifelong habits that had taken root. Over many years, Chris had simply gotten used to everything Alice did, and he took her for granted. It is likely this happens in your marriage in some important ways as well. To understand what this might look like, it will help to identify five specific ways we take each other for granted in our marriages.

## Five Ways We Take Our Partners for Granted

### Expectations

One way we take our partners for granted is in the expectations we set for them. This is a rather insidious and destructive process. It starts in a positive way, with your spouse doing something kind or helpful for you. Maybe it is washing the dishes after dinner or picking up something you needed from the store without being asked. You appreciate the act and are thankful, and you probably say so.

Then it happens again, and you think, *Wow, this is cool. I could get used to this!* Sure enough, that is exactly what you do . . . you get used to it. Over time, what used to be new and exciting becomes the new normal that you now expect. When this happens, you stop noticing and appreciating the things your spouse does, and you take your partner for granted.

Expecting your partner to be loving and kind and do nice things for you is perfectly fine. Getting so used to these acts that you no longer notice them, thank your partner for doing them, or appreciate their value is not fine. No matter how often your spouse performs acts of kindness, *always* notice them, *always* appreciate them, and *always* thank your partner for doing them.

### Decisions

Another way we take our partners for granted is by making decisions that don't include them. Sometimes this happens because you assume you know what your spouse will think. Making assumptions only leads to the "unspoken truths" we covered in chapter 10. Sometimes you may have talked about a decision and known your partner wasn't 100 percent on board, but you went ahead and made the decision anyway.

When you don't ask for help or advice from your spouse, or even for their opinion, you send the message that your partner doesn't matter. I have had more than one couple in my office describe how one of them did not ask the other for an opinion, made a decision on their own, and then had the audacity to blame their partner when the decision didn't work out!

I often tell couples that the process they go through in making a decision is more important than the final decision. You may make a great decision or a poor one, and things may or may not work out as you want. The important thing is that both of you had a part in the decision and believe that your voice was heard on the issue. That way it is almost impossible for one of you to feel taken for granted, as you were both involved in making the decision.

### Lack of Kindness

One of the easiest ways to make your partner feel taken for granted is to stop being kind. When you were dating, perhaps you opened the door and brought your wife flowers. You might have left your husband love notes and did special things for him. Do you find yourself too busy or distracted to take the time to do these things for each other now?

Maybe you show a lack of kindness in the words you use . . . or don't use. You might have said please and thank you more in the past, or perhaps you were softer in your tone of voice. Your partner may notice that you no longer take the time to give compliments. For whatever reason, you just aren't as kind or as courteous with the things you say as you used to be.

One husband I worked with told me, "It's just easier to say hurtful things without thinking about it with Lisa. I know she will forgive me if I say something mean. If I say something like that to my boss, I'll get fired, so I have to be careful. But I know Lisa will forgive me."

This process can become destructive, and your partner can become a punching bag. Somehow, treating your partner in hurtful ways just because you are in a bad mood becomes acceptable. Instead of protecting your partner and being overly kind and considerate, you take advantage of your intimacy and closeness and take out your anger and frustration on the person you love the most.

When you allow yourself to take out your emotions on your partner, you unlock a door to dark places that may be hard to come back from. The damage that is done from this type of controlling, manipulative behavior runs deep. It is repairable, in my opinion, but if you see this pattern in your relationship, I strongly encourage you to consider if professional help might be beneficial.

### Lack of Romance

Romance takes a lot of work in a marriage. Early on in your relationship, you probably invested more time and energy in romance. I have heard couples talk about how important Valentine's Day was to them when they were dating, and now they refer to it as a "Hallmark Holiday." The motivation just isn't there anymore.

Some of you surely make more effort than others, but overall, one of the biggest ways spouses take each other for granted is in the romance department. By the way, the term *romance* covers a lot of area. It involves love, passion, sex, intimacy, trust, kindness, and so much more.

During my years working with couples, they have shared numerous ways in which they have taken each other for granted in this area. Some admit they rarely kiss anymore, and if they do, it is more likely a prelude to sexual contact than an individual act of romance. Others have stopped flirting like they did when they were dating. One wife told me, "That used to be a daily thing, but I haven't flirted with him in years." Others used to be playful and tease each other, but have stopped doing that.

Romance in a marriage doesn't require grand gestures. It often only requires taking the time to say and do things that let your partner know you are thinking of them in a romantic or sexual way. Most marital partners I have worked with want to feel desired, noticed, and appreciated. When this doesn't happen, they can easily start to feel that the romance is gone in the relationship.

### Lack of Time

I remember a comment a husband made during a session years ago. After many attempts in counseling to create space and time for dates for he and his wife, they still were not able to regularly reserve time for each other. He looked at her and said, "I honestly don't know what it will take for us to find time together. This should be so easy. Why can't we do this?"

I will often ask couples I work with to pull out their schedules for the month. Once they have their phones or planners out, I ask them to look at their schedules for the current day and show me where each appears in the other's schedule. Usually, neither partner's name appears in the other's schedule for the day. Then we look at the next week and the next month.

Friends and work colleagues show up, sports activities and the kids show up, the hair stylist and the dentist show up . . . even the dog and some random guy named Frank show up. Sadly, the partner who is supposedly the most important person in their life is absent. Why do we schedule time for strangers but not the people we share our lives with? It doesn't make sense.

Perhaps the most egregious offense in taking one's spouse for granted is the lack of time reserved for your partner and the ease with which that time is sacrificed, even if it has been reserved. When your relationship was brand new, you cherished those moments together and made them a top priority. Where is your marriage on the list of your daily priorities now?

## Three Ways to Prevent Taking Your Partner for Granted

 *Make Time for Three Marriage Moments Every Week*

### Marriage Moment 1: The Schedule

Choose a time when you can sit down together each week for a schedule meeting. Many of the couples I work with choose to spend an hour on Sunday evening, as doing so prepares them for the week. Make a commitment to hold this meeting every week no matter what else comes up.

During this meeting, look over your schedule for the week. Before you set anything else in stone, reserve the next two marriage moments, the check-in and the date, for the coming week. This is important because most couples schedule every other activity before time together. You want to change that pattern and start the week by reserving time for your marriage to grow. If there is not a good work/life balance for either of you for the coming week, adjust the schedule accordingly.

### Marriage Moment 2: The Check-In

The check-in is a time when you can share any concerns or problems that either of you have that you might not be able to bring up at any other time. This scheduled time prevents the pressure of feeling forced to bring up an issue late at night because you now have a moment to talk to each other. An hour is usually more than enough time, as you don't need to resolve every problem you face; you just need a time to bring up issues in a safe, healthy environment.

It is likely that you will each have different issues that are important to you, and you can't cover everything in this midweek meeting. Think of this marriage moment the same way ER nurses look at the crises they face. It is impossible to handle everything all at once, so you have to prioritize and triage the most important issues. You can set up additional times to talk about big issues that come up. The important takeaway message here is that this meeting allows couples to bring hidden issues to light and make the choice to find solutions to them (if possible) rather than ignore them.

### Marriage Moment 3: The Date

A date does not have to include a carriage ride, a candle-light dinner, and a mind-blowing sexual encounter. If you can work them in, that would be awesome, but many weeks may be too busy for an all-out night of romance. I am suggesting that you spend at least two hours every week enjoying time alone together.

A date can be a walk at sunset, a bike ride, dinner, shopping, or sitting quietly together on your patio. Try to avoid activities such as movies or shows in which you can't talk or interact with each other. I recommend that you alternate responsibility for planning the activity each week. This is not a competition to plan the most elaborate date. Creativity counts, of course, as putting in the effort to plan something fun will have its rewards. The most important thing is that you don't let anything interfere with this time together.

I recommend that you put these three marriage moments in red in your planners to indicate they should not be canceled unless there is an emergency. You both have to make a commitment to prioritize these times together every week. This choice is simply too important to overlook; you *must* make these marriage moments a mandatory part of every week.

### Make Decisions Together

Decision making is one aspect of a relationship in which you really see whether a couple is valuing and appreciating each other. Making big decisions together is clearly important, but even small decisions can be problematic if one partner feels left out.

For instance, have you ever had an argument over one partner spending more than the other expected? One suggestion I offer couples is to set a limit for how much one partner can spend without consulting the other. You can each have your own spending money, but when it comes to purchases over a certain amount, you agree not to make those purchases until you talk to each other. Doing so makes both partners feel they are making financial decisions as a team.

In your work lives, you will each make many decisions about your jobs on your own. However, you could agree not to take on additional responsibilities that will involve more hours at work without consulting each other. If something is going to affect the time you have for each other or the stress level in the home, you should make that decision together.

Few decisions *must* be made in the moment. Most things can wait until you talk to each other. If you make the commitment to seek out each other's opinions and learn how decisions will affect both of you, the chances of either of you feeling taken for granted will be much lower.

### Love Each Other Well with Kindness and Respect

Kindness is a daily commitment to treat your partner with the respect, honor, love, and compassion you promised when you said, "I do." This choice is a matter of discipline, commitment, and desire.

Choosing to be kind includes monitoring the tone of voice you use when you speak to your spouse, the attitude you approach your spouse with when you have a disagreement, and the effort you put in to understand your partner's point of view. This means putting your best self forward in all your daily interactions and caring more about how your partner feels than whether or not you get your way in a particular situation.

Think about what you just learned in the chapters on intimacy and unselfishness. All those skills can be used here. Think of your partner's needs before your own, and trust that they will do the same for you. Focus on commitment,

sacrifice, and intimacy as these will help you love your partner well with kindness and respect.

## The Choice Not to Take Each Other for Granted

The choice not to take each other for granted is all about
preventing the deterioration of your relationship. Just like
a healthy garden, a marriage needs to be tended and taken
care of. This is not an easy choice—many of you will need
to reevaluate your priorities. It may take some time to understand how and why you have been making the choice to
ignore so much of what your spouse does for you. But you
should feel a great sense of hope that even if this pattern
has developed in your marriage, it can be changed. All you
have to do is invest the time and energy you have been using
for less important priorities into this new goal—the goal of
building up your partner and letting them know how much
you appreciate all they do each and every day.

Taking each other for granted can destroy your marriage,
but you don't have to let this happen. If you schedule time
for each other, make decisions together, and treat each other
with kindness and respect, you can significantly decrease the
likelihood that you will take each other for granted.

*thirteen*

# I Choose to Focus on the Process

In an episode of one of my favorite shows, *Everybody Loves Raymond*, Ray and his wife, Debra, are fighting over a new can opener that she bought. In the episode, which includes both partners reflecting back on how they remembered the argument, it becomes clear that the fight was never about the can opener.

The episode opens with Ray's mother, who always takes his side, listening intently as Ray describes his perception of how the fight was completely Debra's fault. The scene fades to Ray's memory of how the argument played out, showing him coming home from work, kissing Debra lovingly, and asking her when dinner will be ready. As Debra eats her own dinner, she says she hasn't gotten to making his and that it will be awhile.

Ray calmly starts to make a tuna sandwich for himself, but when using the new can opener Debra bought, he spills tuna juice and eventually drops all the tuna in the sink. When he asks why they needed a new can opener, Debra storms out of the room saying, "This is the new can opener I bought. It's not stupid, and I'm not stupid!" Ray watches her go and says, "What'd I do?"

In stark contrast, Ray's brother, Robert, being perpetually jealous of Ray, eagerly listens to Debra share her version of what Ray did wrong. In her story, Debra describes running around the kitchen trying to feed the kids and attend to their needs when Ray walks in, gruffly snorts a short hello, and demands dinner.

When he learns nothing is ready, he sarcastically says, "Fine. I'll make my own dinner, again." As he opens cabinet doors and slams them shut, he finds a can of tuna is his only option. Looking all over for a can opener, he discovers the new one Debra bought. He attempts to use it, spills a few drops of tuna juice, and begins yelling, "Oh no! Tuna juice!" He soon drops the tuna in the sink while trying to open the can and in the most sarcastic tone possible says, "I would have preferred the tuna on bread, but it's just as good right out of the sink!" Looking at Debra, Ray says, "Did we need a new can opener?" As Debra begins to cry, she says, "This is the new can opener I bought. It's not stupid, and . . . and I . . . I'm not stupid." Ray watches her walk out of the room and says, "What'd I say?"

What really mattered to both Ray and Debra was the way they each felt hurt and disrespected by the other. Ray felt he tried his best to come home and be a part of the family but that Debra was disinterested, angry, and dismissive of him. Debra felt that Ray was rude, insulting, hurtful, and selfish. It wouldn't have mattered if they were fighting over the can opener, his bowling league, the kids, or her job. For most of us, it's not about the can opener.

### Process over Content

Some colleagues in my profession are very content focused. The work they do with clients focuses on specific solutions to specific problems, so they spend a great deal of time working with couples to negotiate compromises or come to resolutions regarding specific issues. I see the value in this approach, but it seems to me that the couples would then need to go through the same intensive process every time a new conflict occurs.

I take a different approach in my work with couples. I believe that process matters much more than content. My clients sometimes get tired of hearing me use the phrase "process over content," but they definitely learn how it applies to their marriages. I don't think a difference in beliefs or attitudes about a certain topic creates conflict between partners; most couples can work through differences of opinion. I think the way they treat each other when they talk about issues causes conflict. In fact, many couples, when they learn to focus on treating each other with respect, honor, and love, sometimes don't even remember what they were arguing about!

In most marriages, when thinking about a disagreement, couples focus on what the disagreement is about. If I were to ask you and your spouse about the last fight you had, both of you would probably describe it by telling me what issue you were disagreeing about. You know, sex, kids, money, in-laws, etc.

I want you to begin thinking about conflict between you and your partner differently. Instead of thinking about conflict in terms of what you fight about, I want you to think about how you treat each other during an argument. Ask yourselves the following questions:

What is your attitude and behavior like?

Are you mean and hurtful, calling each other names, or do you show respect, love, and honor to each other?

Do you interrupt and criticize each other, or do you listen well and focus on your partner?

Do you get distracted and look at your phone or lose focus?

When you argue, does it occur when you are tired or hungry?

Do both of you bring up old issues from the past?

Are you having the argument upriver or right at Niagara Falls?

To help you get a clear view of what "process over content" really looks like, let's take a closer look at the specific elements that make up the process of interacting. Four distinct aspects of how couples interact during a disagreement are central to understanding the process that occurs.

## The Four Pillars of Process

The process I am talking about involves four pillars that can form either a solid foundation that leads to marital harmony

191

or a shaky foundation that leads to marital discord. They involve the way you treat each other, the situation in which the communication takes place, how close to Niagara Falls you are in the conflict process, and your relationship history. The four pillars of process are:

1. Behavior
2. Environment
3. Niagara Falls status
4. Historical context

### Behavior

Process behavior is the way you and your spouse treat each other during a conflict. This pillar includes many aspects of verbal and nonverbal communication. Again, it doesn't matter what topic you are discussing. How you interact with each other and how you treat each other during the discussion have much more to do with the outcome than the content of the discussion.

Verbally, the tone of voice you use has a great deal to do with the process that occurs. If you are sarcastic, derogatory, dismissive, or harsh, the process will not go well. You can refer back to the other negative tones of voice we discussed to remind yourself of the tones of voice to avoid. Other examples of problematic process behavior include interrupting or talking over each other, changing the subject, and raising your voice.

Nonverbally, the attitude you present can directly affect the outcome of the discussion. Many nonverbal gestures have tremendous meaning in our relationships. Crossing your arms in defiance, refusing to look at your partner, and acting disinterested all form a lens through which your message is heard. Other nonverbal actions that create problems are looking at your phone (distracted), raising your eyebrows (dismissive or sarcastic), and shaking your head (disagreeing).

### Environment

The process environment includes the circumstances in which the conflict or disagreement takes place. This pillar includes the location the conflict occurs in, the time of day and time pressure that may exist, and conditions such as being hungry or in a hurry. All these circumstances can greatly affect the way the process plays out.

Location matters a great deal to the process. If you are at home, you may feel comfortable raising your voice or using language that you would not use if you were seated at a nice restaurant. If there are others around, you may be less likely to let the conflict escalate. Some locations can escalate the conflict process, while others can minimize it.

The time of day also matters. To be honest, few successful conflict resolutions take place late at night. When both of you are tired and ready to go to sleep, you won't think as clearly or be as patient as you would during the day. Depending on how quickly you wake up, the same may be true of the early morning. You have to choose a time to interact when you have a good chance of successfully resolving a potential conflict.

There are other environmental factors as well. Don't even consider discussing a difficult topic when you are hungry. It won't work. The same is true for trying to resolve a conflict when one or both of you are late for work or under some other type of time pressure. Wait until you both have had something to eat and have the time to devote to the discussion.

### Niagara Falls Status

The third pillar refers to where you are in the river of relationship conflict. Think back to the Niagara Falls analogy you learned about in chapter 5. Remember all the warning signs you learned to identify so that you would know when you were getting close to the falls? That is what this part of the process is all about.

If you see warning signs that one of you is close to the falls, agree to postpone the discussion until a later time. If you don't recall your warning signs, this is a great time to pull them out and refresh your memory. Knowing how close you are to going over Niagara Falls will help you decide if this is a good time to discuss the issue or not.

You also want to be sure not to start a new conflict cycle if one is already in progress. For instance, if you are already fighting about housework and a new conflict over buying a car develops before the first conflict is resolved, your chances of successful conflict resolution are extremely low. Putting off the car discussion until you resolve the housework issue is more effective.

### Historical Context

The final pillar focuses on the backstory of your relationship and the factors that this particular conflict brings up for each of you. Such factors could include issues from years ago that were never resolved in your relationship.

Other factors include the baggage discussed earlier that one or both of you brought from childhood or previous relationships.

No one comes to a marriage without a backstory that provides context for understanding what is happening in the here and now. The key to this pillar is to be aware of what baggage is being brought up, how it affects your relationship, and what you can do to prevent it from derailing the process completely.

Sometimes the past is so powerful that you have to take a time-out from the current discussion to deal with the issues that are raising their ugly heads. Dealing with your history first so that it doesn't interfere with the current process is beneficial. In fact, you may learn that the backstory to the current conflict is actually causing it. Once you understand the historical context of the issue, you can move on to the issue at hand.

## Process in Action

With almost every husband and wife who allow me to spend time with them, I do my best as a psychologist to help them see the process of what is happening between them. This is sometimes much easier said than done, as the couples I work with don't always want to do this. Sometimes one partner is extremely invested in the issue they bring to the session, and they don't want to let it go.

Keith and RaeLynn had been to only a few sessions with me, and we were still getting to know each other. They had moved to Denver from the Deep South, and many of their interactions had a southern style to them. One evening they came in for their weekly appointment, and as I usually do, I asked them what was on their hearts and minds. This particular evening they clearly had an agenda.

They looked at each other rather intently, with neither speaking for a few seconds. Then Keith opened with, "Do you want to start?"

"Go ahead. You know you want to," RaeLynn answered.

"Okay. Don't say I didn't give you a chance."

RaeLynn just stared back at him and said nothing.

Keith began to talk about an incident that had occurred the night before the session. "It didn't start out as that big of a deal. RaeLynn was making dinner, and the kids were playing in the other room. I was watching TV, like I always do."

RaeLynn said something under her breath.

Keith looked at her and said, "What?"

"Nothing. Go on."

"So as I was saying, it was just a normal night, and then she asked me to set the table. I told her I would, but I forgot. I got involved in the TV show, and then I heard her slamming the silverware down on the table. I had no idea what made her so angry."

RaeLynn looked at him and said rather sarcastically, "Seriously? You're going with that? Whatever . . ."

"Hey, I gave you the chance to talk first, and you told me to go first, and now you keep interrupting me. This is what you always do!"

"Yeah, just like I have to ask you twenty times to get anything done around the house!"

At this point, I decided to offer what I call a "process comment." It is my way of intervening in the interaction in a

196

therapy session to change the focus from content to process. My goal is to interpret what is happening between the couple to provide some context and direction.

"Let's stop for a second here. It seems that neither of you is able to listen well to the other right now. You are almost talking over each other." I went on to suggest a new direction for the conversation. "I would really like to hear both of you share your experience of that night. If I understand correctly, Keith, RaeLynn asked you to set the table and you forgot. Is that correct?"

Keith looked directly at me and said, "So you're going to take her side, Doc?" (Some of my clients call me Doc, but I don't think it is always a term of endearment.)

"Why do you say I'm taking her side? I thought I was just making an observation."

"Well, you just said she was right and I was wrong."

I decided to offer another process comment. "I could be wrong, of course, but it seems that when I make an observation you don't agree with, you can take our difference of opinion personally."

"Look, Doc, you're just missing the point here. I didn't do anything wrong. I came home, watched some TV like I always do after working all day, and just didn't get the table done as fast as she wanted."

RaeLynn, who had been sitting fairly quietly and listening to our conversation, now chimed in. "The real point here is that you never do anything the first time I ask you. I have to ask over and over, and sometimes I just stop asking."

"As usual, it's all my fault," Keith replied sarcastically.

RaeLynn just rolled her eyes. "You see what I have to live with?"

197

## Seeing the Process

Keith felt unfairly accused, and his resentment over this made it difficult for him to hear RaeLynn's experience. He was so distracted by his feelings that he did not have the capacity to see things from her point of view. In fact, he felt so persecuted that he even thought I was taking her side against him.

RaeLynn, on the other hand, was involved in a process that was based on the "unspoken truth" that Keith cared more about himself than her. Her evidence for this was his slow response, or lack of any response, when she asked him to do something at home. She was fighting off a nagging fear that he might not be capable of changing, and because of her disappointment and pain, she had great difficulty expecting him to respond to her in a positive way.

In counseling, I worked with this couple to help them learn to see this process in action and understand what was happening between them. In the therapy sessions, RaeLynn began to see that she had started expecting Keith to fail at caring for her, while Keith realized that he had started expecting her to attack him by telling him how he had failed. They both learned to identify baggage from their families of origin and previous relationships that had contributed to their current relational process with each other.

You can learn to understand the interactions that occur in your marriage as well. Instead of trying to fix every conflict or resolve specific problems, you can learn how to see and understand the process that happens between the two of you. When you learn to do this, you don't have to start from scratch with every disagreement or conflict. Instead, you can focus on developing a solid, positive, healthy process in your relationship for handling whatever issues develop.

## EXERCISE
## Focusing on Process over Content

To learn how to focus on process over content in your marriage, complete the following exercise. It will help you work on three specific skills: paying more attention to the way you and your spouse are feeling, paying less attention to the topic of the discussion, and changing the way you treat each other.

### Step 1: Focus on Each Other

To start this exercise, choose a topic that you have a difference of opinion about. It could be an area of conflict you would like to address or a decision you have to make. Just make sure it is a topic you disagree about but that you are both still able to talk openly about with each other.

Choose a comfortable time and place and start discussing the issue. However, while you are listening to your partner or sharing your views, see if you can multitask. Attempt to pay attention to how you are feeling and how your partner is feeling. Notice things such as how you feel when your partner disagrees with you and what you see in your partner's body language when you disagree.

Pay attention to whether your tone of voice is as kind when you or your partner are sharing an alternative point of view as when you are agreeing. Are you feeling upset? Hurt? Ignored? Angry? Try to focus more on the emotions that you are both feeling than on the point-counterpoint of the discussion.

The Niagara Falls approach is valuable here. Do you see any warning signs that tell you the falls are getting close? Are you able to step back from the discussion and point out those warning signs to each other, or do you blow right past them?

The goal here is to become skilled at having a conversation about a topic you disagree on while paying close attention to the process of how you are communicating. This is necessary for the next step, as you must be aware of what is happening in your relationship if you want to maintain healthy, positive communication. Don't move on to the next step until you both agree you have been able to complete this first step.

### Step 2: Focus Less on the Topic

Now that you are paying close attention to what is happening between the two of you, you can move on to the topic you are discussing. In the past, both of you likely focused on what you thought about the topic. In fact, as soon as you both chose the topic for this exercise, you may have mentally started creating a list of the points you wanted to make. You may even have come up with a plan in your mind for how you could "win" the argument.

Do you remember the active listening exercise from chapter 3? From this exercise, you each learned to restate what the other said and accurately understand what was being communicated. That skill set will help you in this task. Focus on what your partner is saying and on understanding it correctly rather than thinking about what you want to say in response.

In fact, an excellent goal for this part of the exercise is to try to make statements that reflect your partner's point of view rather than arguing points of your own. If you both do this and try to clarify how your partner feels, you will quickly lose the desire to win and will focus on understanding each other instead.

If you want your partner to feel heard, understood, and cared for, focus more on the process of what is happening between you than on the content of the actual issue. Of course, some discussions will lead to a decision, but that is not necessary during this exercise. The goal is to learn to focus more on each other rather than on the issue.

### Step 3: Change What You Need to Change

The last step in this exercise is to talk through what you learned from it. Ask each other how well you were able to focus on the process of your interactions instead of the content of the discussion. Tell each other what you noticed in yourself that you would like to work on and see if your partner noticed the same thing. Make suggestions to each other about what you would like your partner to consider changing that would help the process go more smoothly. Be as honest as you can about yourself and your partner.

Once you have completed this discussion, you can choose to end the exercise, or you can return to the discussion if there is more to say. If you return to the discussion, you can practice working on the things you shared with each other, or you can work on them the next time you discuss an issue. These changes will help you value process over content in your marriage.

## The Choice to Focus on Process over Content

To make this a permanent change in your marriage, take note of the tendencies you each have and how these play out in the relationship. Look for communication issues that repeat themselves and thoughts, behaviors, and reactions that increase conflict between the two of you. The more you learn about your go-to strategies for responding to each other, the easier it will be to see the warning signs and get out of the water before you go over the falls.

As you both become skilled at seeing the process that takes place between you, the content of specific issues will become less important. You will find that your relationship will grow by leaps and bounds when you both begin to care more about treating each other with respect and dignity than winning an argument.

I don't have to work that hard to sell you on this choice, do I? It's the whole teach a man to fish principle. If you can learn to choose to relate to your spouse in healthy ways, then you will be able to handle whatever issues create difficulty for you in the future. This choice will be the proverbial gift that keeps on giving, as you will see it pay dividends for years to come.

*fourteen*

# I Choose to Trust

Trust is one of the biggest challenges many couples face. Some of you have experienced betrayal in your marriage due to infidelity, lying, or other conflicts. Here is the thing about trust. It takes a long time to build, but it can be destroyed in an instant. Trust is the bedrock of every marriage relationship. When trust is strong, you can handle almost anything life throws your way. However, when trust is broken, the foundation breaks apart, and nothing seems stable.

Choosing to trust your spouse means taking risks and allowing yourself to be vulnerable. You could get hurt if your partner lets you down, and that can be really scary. The upside to trusting your partner is that the intimacy you develop is something you will never experience at any other time in your life. As you learned in the chapter on intimacy, being truly known by another human being is one of the most rewarding experiences of life, and this can't happen without trust.

## EXERCISE
# Remembering Your Wedding Vows

Trust is all about keeping our promises. Ngina Otiende said the following: "A great marriage is made up of two people who consistently put their vows before their feelings."[1] Think about that for a moment. If that statement is true, then the promises you made to your partner when you got married should be driving every choice you make in your relationship. There is a reason why the central feature of every wedding ceremony is the vows the man and woman make to each other.

When you made those vows, though, how well did you know your partner? Sure, you may have dated for a few months or even a few years, but as time passes in a marriage, you learn so much more about each other. You begin to realize that your relationship has to be based on principles that drive the choices you make.

Have your marriage vows served as a set of core principles that are the bedrock of your marriage? Some couples I work with don't even remember what their marriage vows were. If you can't recite your marriage vows by memory, how important can they be to the choices you make in your relationship?

To begin this exercise, go find your marriage vows. Then read them out loud to each other. Read them slowly and clearly. Listen carefully to the promises you made. Have you kept those promises? Do you even remember all of them, or were they just words you haven't looked at in years?

After you have read them out loud, consider each promise one at a time. Talk to each other about how well you have been able to keep each promise. If you have done well in keeping a promise, talk about how you have succeeded and why. If you have not been able to keep a promise, think through the reasons it has been a challenge and talk about how you can improve in this area.

The next part of this exercise focuses on the future. Now that you have completed a thorough evaluation of your marriage vows and agreed on how well you have done in keeping the promises you made, it is time to set some specific goals. Identify the vows that have been a challenge for each of you individually and those that have been difficult as a couple.

For each of the vows that have proven difficult, develop a plan for what each partner will do individually and what you will do together as a couple to keep it. For instance, if you promised not to take each other for granted, but you have done so often, you could promise to make daily affirmations to each other. You could start keeping a gratitude journal of all the things you appreciate about each other, or you could set aside one night each week to spend together as a couple.

The goal here is to create a clear plan that will help you keep the marriage vows you made. Remember what you have learned as you will need this information in chapter 15. In that chapter, I will ask you to consider the benefits of having a formal ceremony in which you renew your vows, and this exercise helps you prepare for that discussion.

## The Four Building Blocks of Trust

In my work with couples, and in my own marriage, I have discovered four building blocks that form the basis for real and lasting trust in a marriage. As we examine these building blocks, you will see how they work together to form a trusting marital relationship. These are the conditions under which trust can grow and flourish in a marriage.

### Honesty

It may seem as if I am being Captain Obvious here, but trust starts with honesty. Everyone understands that major betrayals, such as an affair, have a huge effect on trust in a marriage, and most people believe there is room for a few little white lies in every marriage to protect a partner's feelings. As we discussed previously, small lies lead to big lies. A pattern can develop when couples lie about things or hide information on a regular basis.

Your grandmother probably told you that honesty is the best policy. If you don't follow her advice, it is most likely because you fear the consequences of telling the truth. There is no reason to lie if you are certain telling the truth won't cause a problem, right? Some of you may lie to protect someone's feelings, out of guilt, to avoid a conflict, or to prevent others from seeing the real you. But you probably lie most often because you are worried about what will happen if you tell the truth.

Psychologist Martin Seligman called this "learned helplessness." He studied how dogs reacted to receiving an electrical shock. As this was before the protection of animals in research studies, he was able to allow one group of dogs to prevent the shock while the other group could not prevent it. He learned that when dogs were unable to prevent a bad thing, such as an electrical shock, they gave up trying to prevent it and just accepted that it was going to happen. They didn't make any attempts to avoid it and just lay down and waited to be shocked. He called this learned helplessness because they learned to quit trying to help themselves.[2]

This same principle applies to marriage. If you have tried to be honest in your relationship but that attempt has been met with anger or hurtfulness, you may be hesitant to be honest in the future. If you have been burned several times by being honest, you may be tempted to give up on it completely.

Here is the thing I want you to consider. Why would you settle for a marriage based on lies and deceit, or even one based on avoiding the truth? I understand why you would be afraid of being hurt again, but doesn't it make more sense to fix the problem? If you deal with your partner's reaction and overcome that problem, you won't have to keep avoiding it.

When you choose honesty in your marriage, you are choosing to have a voice in your relationship and to speak the truth even if it might be uncomfortable. You are not doing your partner any favors by allowing their emotional reaction to prevent you from being honest. Having the difficult conversations shows your spouse that you care about a truly authentic relationship.

### Integrity

*Merriam-Webster's Collegiate Dictionary* defines *integrity* as "firm adherence to a code of especially moral or artistic values; incorruptibility."[3] Integrity is all about who you are as a person—what you stand for and what defines the decisions you make. Integrity is a matter of keeping your promises and simply doing what you say you will do.

John Wooden once said, "Be more concerned with your character than your reputation, because your character is what you really are, while your reputation is merely what others *think* you are."[4] You can talk about having character all you want, but integrity is seen in your deeds—not your words.

Here are some questions you can ask yourself to determine your level of integrity:

Are you a person of your word?

When you tell your partner you will do something, do you do it or not?

If your friends and family were interviewed, would they say you are a person of integrity?

When you promise to do something, do you make keeping that commitment a priority?

When you make a promise, do you try to think of ways to get out of the commitment?

Do you have a moral code that guides your choices?

What would you say are the defining elements of your character?

Are you honest in your daily interactions with others?

Your answers to these questions form the basis of whether you are a person of integrity. There is no hiding from these answers, as they are based on the choices you have made in the past. If this is an area you struggle with, you may not have integrated a moral code into your life that guides your daily decisions.

Several things contribute to the development of a personal moral or ethical code. For some, their religious faith provides these tenets based on a book such as the Bible or the Koran. Others learned these principles from their parents or people they respected and admired. Still others define their moral code based on their life experiences and the consequences of choices they have made.

208

In my years working as a federal prison psychologist, I came to realize that most of the inmates I worked with did not have a clear moral code. Lawrence Kohlberg developed six stages of moral reasoning, and the highest stage involved using a set of moral principles or codes to make decisions.[5] However, most of the guys I spent time working with in prison made choices based on whether they were likely to get caught and what the punishment would be if they were.

If you want to be a person of integrity in your marriage, you have to stand for something. Choose your moral code carefully, as your decisions will flow out of those principles. If you are a person of integrity, your partner will know you will honor your promises, and this is a huge step toward building trust in a marriage.

### Reliability

Once you have established honesty and integrity in your relationship, the next building block of trust involves maintaining these qualities over a long period of time. Reliability is the dependable, consistent, and steadfast application of principles such as honesty and integrity over the long haul and in all types of situations. If your partner can begin to expect you to show these qualities on a regular basis, much more often than not, you are well on your way to building trust in your marriage.

We are talking about having each other's back here. When your partner needs you, you are there. They can depend on you to tell the truth and keep your promises regardless of the circumstances you are facing. Reliable people show up and keep showing up when the ones they love need them. They rarely make excuses, so you won't hear a reliable person say,

"I would have been there for you, but . . ." or "I would have told you the truth, but . . ." Reliable people simply know the right thing to do and do it.

You want that type of reliability from your partner, right? So why wouldn't you give every bit of effort possible to be that person for your partner? If you choose to value your partner over yourself, then being a partner who is reliable, honest, and a person of integrity makes complete sense. What often trips people up in the pursuit of this goal is their own selfish desires. We would have little difficulty being reliable if we weren't worried about consequences and other people's opinions.

### Vulnerability

The last building block for a solid foundation of trust for your marriage is vulnerability. This involves allowing your spouse to get close to you and believing that she or he will be there for you when needed. For you to become vulnerable with your partner, you have to let down your defenses. This may be scary as they have served you well in the past. And choosing to be vulnerable is risky—you can and often do get hurt. Making the choice to be vulnerable means that you are taking the chance your partner may not have your back.

However, vulnerability is a step toward your partner and provides the opportunity for your spouse to make the right choice and be there when you need support—to actually come through for you.

Choosing to look toward the future and believing in your spouse and your marriage create a backdrop for building trust. Making the choice to be vulnerable opens you to new levels of connection and intimacy with your spouse. The result? Real, lasting trust with your life partner.

## David and Gloria

I have worked with many couples like David and Gloria, whose trust had been broken due to financial issues. Gloria described the conflict they were having by saying, "He won't let me buy anything. If I go shopping, he wants to see the receipts and know everything I bought. Then he starts telling me how we didn't really need this or that and how I'm wasting money."

David, on the other hand, felt the financial pressure was all on him. "I have to pay the bills myself because she kept paying them late or missing some. All the pressure is on me to make enough money to pay the bills and keep us above water."

Gloria bristled at this, saying, "I work hard too, you know. I work full-time *and* take care of the kids and the house. I don't see you helping much with that. And by the way, I try really hard to help out with the bills and the financial stuff whenever I can. You just don't trust me to do it."

One evening, David came to a session and talked about a recent argument. He had asked for Gloria's help with moving some money from one account to another, and Gloria had agreed to take care of it. A few days later, David happened to check the account balance, and it was overdrawn because Gloria had forgotten to move the money.

David hated it when the checking account was overdrawn. It embarrassed him, and paying overdraft fees drove him nuts. More importantly, he was frustrated that Gloria hadn't done what she had said she would.

In the moments after he found out what had happened, he was faced with a choice between grace and criticism. Unfortunately, in this instance, David chose poorly. He stayed

211

with anger and frustration, feeling mistreated and unheard. As soon as Gloria got home, he let her have it. No soft tones, no compassion. He led the conversation with "This is why I can't trust you to pay the bills. You don't take it seriously. If this mattered to you, you would have moved that money."

When I saw them in the office, they hadn't spoken for two days. Gloria didn't say much, as she already felt she had failed him. She sat quietly, looking as if she wanted to cry but refusing to do so, while David told the story of what had happened the week before.

To his credit, David didn't defend his actions. He just looked at Gloria, defeated and broken down, and sighed. "I messed up again," he said quietly. "I guess I took out my anger on her."

I looked at him calmly and in my best Dr. Phil voice asked, "How's that working for you?"

He just smiled wryly and said, "That's why we're here."

David wasn't a bad guy. In fact, he loved Gloria and was not so different from many husbands I know. You might not think so from this part of his story, but he had a good heart and wanted to make his marriage work. However, his priorities clearly needed readjusting, as his choices were making Gloria feel distrusted, incompetent, unimportant, and unloved.

We started with small choices in the area of trust. I supported David in his efforts to learn to trust Gloria to make financial decisions on her own. I also suggested that Gloria think carefully about what she agreed to do for David and then follow through on those things. They created lists of what financial choices were most important and identified specific behaviors they each wanted to change the most.

David and Gloria realized that they could learn to change the way they thought about their choices, consider consequences before they acted, and then make different choices. This was a completely new experience for them, but it took only a few weeks for them to see the difference in the level of trust in their relationship. In the space of a few months, they began to believe these changes would become a permanent transformation in their marriage.

## The Choice to Trust

If trust is solid and secure in your relationship, the skills in this chapter will help you maintain it. However, for those readers who are trying to make the choice to rebuild trust after an affair or some other betrayal, I have three specific suggestions for you.

First, go back and reread chapter 7 on forgiving the big stuff. Much of that chapter is directly relevant to building trust in your marriage.

Second, consider working with a marriage counselor or psychologist. A licensed, trained, and experienced therapist can help you interpret what has happened between the two of you. They can help you both understand the dynamics that led to a loss of trust, rebuild the broken parts of the relationship, and begin the journey forward.

Finally, both of you need to make the choice to be all in. If you were the partner who betrayed your spouse, you need to take personal responsibility for your actions and make whatever changes are needed to prevent it from happening again. If you are the partner who was betrayed, you have to make the choice to stop holding on to resentment and bitterness—to give up the power and control they create. You may even need to consider what role you might have had in the state of the relationship prior to the betrayal.

The choice to trust involves many of the previous choices you have learned to make. It includes letting go of the past, forgiving each other, and believing in the hope of a better relationship. It is not a choice to forget what happened but a choice to learn from your experience and grow even stronger in the future.

# *fifteen*

# I Choose to Love You Forever

The choice to love each other is up to you. You have learned about ten choices that can transform your marriage forever. The exercises in this book have provided opportunities for you to put these choices into practice and understand how they apply to your unique marriage relationship.

This last chapter offers you the final pieces to the puzzle. You need to be able to make these changes permanent. They should become second nature in your day-to-day decisions. You need to have a strong commitment to making these choices regardless of the stage of life in which you find yourself. To this end, this chapter offers some suggestions for making these choices permanent.

First, we will review the key points of each chapter. This review will remind you of the tools you now have. Each choice provides a different opportunity for permanent change in your marriage.

After this review, we will look at two examples of how your season of life can affect the choices you make. Through two final stories from couples (one a fictional TV family and another based on a real family), you will learn how important it is to understand the effect your stage of life has on your choices.

Next, you will complete an exercise that will help you finalize the choices you started to make earlier in the book regarding the specific core principles you want to be central in your marriage. Through developing a marital coat of arms that lays out the values you choose to commit to, you will create a clear picture of the principles on which future choices can be made.

Finally, you will consider the possibility of participating in a public or private renewal of vows ceremony that would allow you to make an authentic commitment to these choices for the future. We will review the important elements of such a ceremony and discuss the many benefits it can offer. This final step in the commitment process is often one of the most significant and transformational steps in a couple's marital growth.

## → The Highlights

In chapter 2, you made the choice to believe. Allowing yourself to have some small wins gave you the ability to have hope for the future. Learning to expect success helped you interrupt negative patterns from the past and remember that success is possible. You also learned to pay attention to positive experiences and use them to expect the future to be brighter.

In chapter 3, you chose to communicate accurately. By practicing the ABCs of communication and improving your

216

communication accuracy, brevity, clarity, and delivery, you significantly improved your ability to understand each other. Using bullet points, changing negative tones of voice, and making clear statements, you are now able to have productive conversations without conflict. In chapter 4, you chose to communicate positively through learning about positive praise, positive leadership, and positive coaching. You learned to use the ten rules for positive communication to strengthen and improve communication in your marriage.

When you got to chapter 5, you made the choice to let go of old baggage. By considering the baggage you both brought to the relationship from your families of origin and previous romantic relationships, you learned why some of the patterns in your relationship occur. Specific skills, such as taking a time-out and avoiding the falls, provided clear steps for changing these patterns.

Chapters 6 and 7 helped you make the choice to forgive. You learned the dangers of unforgiveness and strategies for forgiving the big stuff. Understanding how to share power in the relationship, realizing that marriage is not always fair, and seeing the value of repentance helped you look at forgiveness in a new light. Whether you have had an incident of betrayal in your marriage or not, you learned that affairs, financial issues, lying, and selfishness can be overcome with a healthy and authentic forgiveness process.

In chapters 8 and 9, you made the decision to choose unselfishness. You took some time to understand the complex issues involved with this process, including the value that sacrifice and commitment provide in a marriage. You learned to rethink your process of making decisions as a couple and to look at your model of marriage. You took the selfishness quiz and discovered the value that the "us" marriage model provides when compared with the "me" marriage model.

When you arrived at chapter 10, you chose to challenge "unspoken truths." This involved learning about the assumptions you and your partner have made in the relationship, sometimes over many years. By understanding these "unspoken truths," you learned about underlying beliefs you each had about the other that may have had a powerful effect on your relationship without you even knowing it.

Chapter 11 led you to make the choice to be intimate. After taking the time to understand what intimacy involves and the power that being known can bring to a relationship, you chose to build intimacy. You did this through simple acts of kindness, a positive and encouraging attitude, touch, talking about sex, and sharing inside stories.

In chapter 12, you chose not to take each other for granted. You learned to be aware of when this is happening by "noticing the door." You discovered five ways you can take each other for granted: expectations, decisions, lack of kindness, lack of romance, and lack of time. You also learned three ways to prevent this from happening.

In chapter 13, you chose to focus on process over content. This new skill allowed you to understand that conflicts are often "not about the can opener" and that the process of interacting in your relationship is what matters. You discovered the four pillars of process (behavior, environment, Niagara Falls status, and historical context) and found that you can use these to prevent marital discord.

In chapter 14, you chose to trust. Both of you returned to the marriage vows you made to each other and reconsidered those promises. You came to understand how the four building blocks of trust (honesty, integrity, reliability, and vulnerability) can be used to establish trust or help trust grow in your marriage.

## Seasons of a Marriage

Life looks different during different seasons of a marriage. The choices you make will be highly influenced by the stage of life in which you find yourself. Let's look at two specific seasons, the adolescent years and the empty nest, and how they may affect the choices we have discussed.

### The Child-Raising Years

Raising kids is hard. That's all there is to it. Many books have been written about how to parent, but sometimes you wonder if the authors ever had a child. Each child is unique, and multiple children mean multiple issues. It's just really difficult to make the choices you need to make for your marriage with all the complications that raising children present.

My wife and I are big fans of the TV show *The Middle*. The show takes place in a small town in the heartland of America (Orson, Indiana). The show centers on the Heck family—Mike and Francine "Frankie" Heck and their three children, Axl, Sue, and Brick. Axl is the typical Millennial boy, focused on athletics, girls, or anything but academics, while Sue is an awkward young lady with a good heart who is just trying to fit in. The youngest boy, Brick, has a variety of eccentric behaviors that create significant social and family conflict.

The marital relationship is typical of many. Mike is a blue-collar quarry worker who just wants to come home and relax after a hard day of work, but he is usually met with a variety of conflicts from Frankie and the kids. Frankie, for her part, balances working full-time with trying to take care of the house and the needs of her husband and kids.

Jan and I love this show because it portrays so many of the daily challenges we have faced as parents. The Heck family can't seem to get through an hour, let alone a day, without some type of sibling fight or parenting conflict that requires intervention.

In one classic episode, the family decides to go to the movies. Between Axl having a conflict with the friend he brings to the movie, Sue running into a boy she had a crush on who has now decided to become a priest, and Brick stealing a movie sign that offends him, the family has little time to enjoy the movie. As with most episodes of the show, Mike and Frankie face a choice as marital partners and parents. Mike thinks Frankie interrupted him when he tried to tell a story to some of his friends. By itself, this would have been a mild disagreement in which his feelings got hurt. Mike would tell Frankie how he felt, she would apologize, and he would forgive her.

However, when this incident occurred on the heels of several other family conflicts, it resulted in a blowup. Mike was mad at Frankie, Frankie was mad at Mike, and they both took their frustrations out on the kids. With the stress of all three children already pushing them to the limit, they chose to fight with each other instead of giving each other the benefit of the doubt.

The stress of raising children and balancing work and home can make it difficult to choose wisely as a couple. I suggest that you be aware of these stressors during this season of your marriage and make the following allowances. First, before you go over the falls, stop to ask if the situation that occurred was caused by or related to being parents. If so, give each other a break and don't make each other collateral damage for a problem that belongs to the kids.

Second, if you are dealing with challenges due to being parents, resolve those issues first before you begin to address any marital conflict. In many situations, the conflict you *think* you have may actually not exist, as resolving the parenting issue may resolve the marital issue.

Finally, allow some space and time for dealing with parenting issues apart from your relationship. You may need to add another Marriage Moment that is specifically focused on dealing with issues revolving around raising children. This season of life has limited bandwidth for conflict resolution on its own without further limiting your capacity. Accept the reality of this period in your life by giving each other the grace and understanding you both deserve.

### The Empty Nest

As difficult as making relational choices can be when you are faced with the challenges of having children, choosing to love each other well can be just as difficult after the kids are gone. Here is an example of the difficulties couples face once all the kids have moved away and the empty-nest season begins.

Cleo and Walter had a strong and stable marriage in many ways. They had been married over thirty years and had raised three kids together, all of whom had launched and showed no signs of returning to the nest. They both enjoyed successful careers, hers in higher education and his in small business ownership. These careers were both drawing to a close as they had prepared well financially and were ready to retire.

It wasn't until the kids left home that they sensed the underlying problem with intimacy that had always been there. While their lives had been full with building careers and raising kids, there had been little time left over to devote to intimacy and closeness in their marriage. With careers drawing to a close and kids out on their own, they felt like strangers living in the same house.

Walter and Cleo realized most of their conversations over the years had been about the kids and their jobs. The conversations about the future they could recall were mostly related to financial planning. They couldn't remember how to share their feelings or hopes for the future, and they had forgotten how to have fun together.

The child-rearing season of their lives had taken its toll on their relationship. They had made good coparents and career professionals, but the price had been the loss of intimacy and trust. It may sound strange, but what proved to be the most helpful to this couple was that I offered interventions in counseling that basically amounted to premarital therapy.

We spent some sessions talking about who they each were as people—their needs and desires, personality styles, hopes and dreams for the future, and strengths and weaknesses. It became clear that they knew very little about each other outside of their parenting styles and career skills. We actually spent most of our counseling sessions introducing them to each other and discussing what they each wanted their future together to look like. This proved to be extremely helpful in adjusting to their new season of life.

Keeping your marital priorities straight during the seasons of your marriage can be difficult. Whether it is the pressure of raising kids, the challenges presented by career opportunities, or the difficulties found in empty nesting and retirement, the seasons of a marriage complicate choices in marriage.

One way to focus your priorities is to make a clear and long-lasting commitment to specific characteristics in your relationship that will weather the storms the seasons of a marriage bring. The following exercise will help you do that.

## A Marital Coat of Arms

In medieval times, around the twelfth century, lords and knights began using a coat of arms to represent themselves. Many Europeans continued this tradition of heraldry, with some developing a family coat of arms that was often referred to as a family crest. These crests or coats of arms displayed what the family stood for, with each color and symbol having a specific meaning. The characteristics of the family and the principles it stood for were all represented, including concepts such as honor, hope, forgiveness, strength, patience, and humility.

I strongly recommend that you develop a marital coat of arms that lays out exactly what the two of you stand for and the principles on which your choices will be made. As you worked your way through this book, you should both have begun to crystalize some principles that you want to form the bedrock of your marriage. The ten choices you have learned in this book and the knowledge you have gained about each other through the exercises you have completed provide a myriad of concepts to choose from.

223

## EXERCISE
## Creating a Marital Coat of Arms

Before I explain this exercise, may I make a small request? You could complete this task in a very basic way, with only minimal effort, and move on to the many demands you have in your life. I want to encourage you not to take that approach. This opportunity is too important.

I ask that you set aside an hour or two each week over the next few weeks. You don't have to finish this exercise right now. Feel free to take plenty of time to think through this challenging task to make sure what you come up with is authentic, well considered, and mutually agreed on. The principles you choose in this exercise will guide your relationship for years to come. Take the time to do this right.

Start by finding a comfortable place to talk. Think about the places you have been creative in the past, and choose one of those places. This exercise will involve thinking about your hopes and dreams for the future and what principles you want your marriage to be based on.

For this first step, you will need a large sheet of paper and colored pens or a dry erase board and some colored markers. On the paper or the board, in one color, write down any words that come to mind that describe the way you would like your relationship to be. Here are some questions you can think about as you complete this part of the task:

If you were listening in on a conversation in which your friends were describing your marriage, what would you hope to hear?

What are the characteristics you aspire to in your marriage and the qualities you want your marriage to embody?

What words describe the way you want to treat each other, how you make decisions, how you raise your children, how you serve your community, and how you live your lives?

You can use the ten choices from this book as a guideline for some of the terms you choose. Write down as many words as the two of you can come up with that honestly and accurately describe the way you want to live out your marriage. You don't have to agree on the words at this point; any word that one of you wants to write down is fine.

Next, with this big list in front of you, narrow down the list to ten words. You can decide on this together as a couple, or you can take turns circling one word in another color that you feel is at the top of your list so both partners select their five top choices.

After you have circled your top ten choices, look at the list and the words you left off. Are there any words you would like to substitute? Work together as a team at this point to come up with a final list.

Now take a new sheet of paper or erase the board and start over. If you are using a dry erase board, I highly recommend you take a picture of the full list of terms before you erase it. Those other words are important and may come in handy later in your marriage.

Write down the final ten words you have chosen for your marital coat of arms, leaving plenty of room to write around each word. As a couple, work together to define each word. Write down what it means to each of you and clearly identify what the concept would look like in your relationship.

Next, come up with pictures or images that represent each word. For instance, if you chose the word *fairness*, you might use a picture of a scale that is equally balanced. Choose an image that represents each word well. Again, you don't have to do this quickly; take time to come up with images that matter.

Now that you have the words and images that will represent your marriage in the future, it is time to create your marital coat of arms. To do this, you simply need to be as creative as you would like to be. The goal is to translate the words and images into an artistic creation that you can place in your home.

You can draw, make something out of wood, or use arts and crafts supplies. Any type of creative endeavor is acceptable. It is important to do this part of the exercise together so that you both can take ownership of and be proud of what you produce. When you are done, you will have created a truly unique and memorable piece of artwork that will serve as a reminder of what you want your marital relationship to stand for.

## Renewal of Vows Ceremony

You are nearing the end of the journey this book has taken you on. However, there is one final step I want you to consider taking. In the previous chapter, I asked you to contemplate your wedding vows again and told you that we'd be using them for one final task.

When you first made your marriage vows to each other, you honestly didn't know everything you were getting into. None of us did. No matter how long you dated or were engaged, actually living together and keeping those marriage vows is a whole different ball game.

Many couples I have worked with have chosen to take part in a ceremony that celebrates new vows they have made to each other after the work they have done in therapy. They know so much more about each other, have chosen to put the past behind them and look forward, and are different people than they were when they first said, "I do."

This can be an incredibly meaningful and touching ceremony that memorializes the changes you have made and the commitments you are making for the future. There are no specific road maps for what a vow renewal ceremony has to look like. However, a couple of general guidelines may make your decision about this step a bit easier.

First, this ceremony can be either public or private. I have seen it work wonderfully either way. Some couples want family and friends to be aware of the changes they have made and would like these individuals to hold them accountable, so they include them in the celebration and commitments. They may want to have a formal ceremony with a pastor, perhaps in a church or a location similar to that of their original wedding.

Others may feel more comfortable spending a romantic weekend together and sharing their vows in a special, private time. Still others may have a small ceremony with a couple of close friends and some important family members present. Regardless of the type of ceremony, the important thing is that it celebrates the new commitments you are making to each other.

Second, you both should seriously consider what vows you now want to make. I encourage spouses to think carefully about the things they have learned about each other and themselves and to identify the specific new promises they want to make to each other. This is why I recommend that you complete your marital coat of arms first, as that exercise will show you what principles you are choosing to make priorities in your marriage.

The new vows should address the authentic story of your relationship and the specific promises you want to make to each other now that you have taken the time to explore your story. You can use the ten choices from this book, as many of these choices form the basis for specific promises you may want to make to each other in the future. You can also use what you learned in the wedding vows exercise in chapter 14. The important thing is that your vows are clear, specific, and measurable promises that you can hold yourself (and each other) accountable for.

The renewal of vows ceremony serves two primary purposes. First, it is an opportunity to clarify what you have learned about the choices you face in your relationship and to make clear, specific promises about the choices you agree to make in the future. Second, it is also a chance to celebrate the hard work you have both done in the process of working to transform your marriage.

For both of these reasons, I believe the final step in transforming your marriage is to take part in a renewal of vows ceremony. It cements the changes you are making while allowing you to celebrate the choice to transform your marriage into the relationship you always dreamed of. Completing this ceremony will be a choice you definitely will not regret.

## The End of All Things

In the final scene of the Lord of the Rings trilogy, Frodo and Samwise have completed their quest and are sitting together on the edge of the destruction of Mt. Doom. As they share a few final moments before what they assume will be the end of their lives, they take turns reminiscing about the Shire and the future that might have been. Frodo looks at Samwise and says, "I'm glad to be with you, Samwise Gamgee, here at the end of all things."

But as those of you who are fans of the series know, it was not the "end of all things." Gandalf flies in on the wings of eagles to rescue them both. Frodo awakens to find Gandalf, Merry and Pippin, Gimli, Legolas, Aragorn, and all those who had shared his journey waiting for him. His story was not over; in fact, it was just the beginning of yet another chapter in the great saga of his life.

And so it is for you in your marriage. This is not the end of your story—it is just the beginning of a brand-new chapter in the grand narrative of your life together. So much of your story has yet to be written.

The one truth that has been woven throughout this entire book is that the choices you make can transform your marriage into the relationship you have always dreamed of. You have the power to choose.

You can choose to hope and believe . . . to communicate well . . . to let go of old baggage . . . to forgive . . . to be unselfish . . . to challenge "unspoken truths" . . . to be intimate . . . to not take each other for granted . . . to choose process over content . . . and to trust. You can choose . . . to love. Make the decision to write a new chapter in the great story of your lives, and choose to love each other forever.

# Notes

## Chapter 1 Marriage Is about Choices

1. William Glasser, *Choice Theory: A New Psychology of Personal Freedom* (New York: HarperCollins, 1999).

2. William Samuelson and Richard Zeckhauser, "Status Quo Bias in Decision Making," *Journal of Risk and Uncertainty* 1, no. 1 (March 1988): 7–59.

3. Alexander Kempf and Stefan Ruenzi, "Status Quo Bias and the Number of Alternatives: An Empirical Illustration from the Mutual Fund Industry," *CFR Working Paper*, no. 05–07 (2005): 1–29.

4. Nikki Sellers, "Had a Row with Your Partner Today? That'll Be One of the 2,455 You Will Have This Year," *Daily Mail*, updated May 20, 2011, http://www.dailymail.co.uk/news/article-1389002/Fallout-Couples -argue-average-seven-times-day.html.

5. Sellers, "Had a Row with Your Partner Today?"

6. Sellers, "Had a Row with Your Partner Today?"

7. Sellers, "Had a Row with Your Partner Today?"

8. John Gottman and Nan Silver, "What Makes Marriage Work?" *Psychology Today*, March 1, 1994, https://www.psychologytoday.com /articles/200910/what-makes-marriage-work.

9. Ken Johnson, "The Good and Bad of Conflict," Mediate.com, August 2014, http://www.mediate.com/articles/JohnsonK6.cfm.

10. *Merriam-Webster's Collegiate Dictionary*, 11th ed. (2008), s.v. "conflict."

## Chapter 2 I Choose to Believe

1. John Ayto, *Dictionary of Word Origins* (New York: Arcade, 1993), s.v. "hope."

2. *Merriam-Webster's Collegiate Dictionary*, s.v. "hope."

3. Theodore W. Schwartz, *Clearing the Land Mines of Marriage: The Intergenerational Causes of Marital Conflict* (Bloomington, IN: Trafford, 2006), ii.

## Chapter 3 I Choose to Communicate Well: Part 1

1. Mind Tools Content Team, "Active Listening: Hear What People Are Really Saying," Mind Tools, accessed June 25, 2018, https://www.mindtools.com/CommSkll/ActiveListening.htm.

2. Harville Hendrix, *Getting the Love You Want: A Guide for Couples*, 20th anniversary ed. (New York: Henry Holt & Company, 2007).

## Chapter 4 I Choose to Communicate Well: Part 2

1. Gottman and Silver, "What Makes Marriage Work?"

2. Gary Chapman, *The 5 Love Languages: The Secret to Love That Lasts* (Chicago: Northfield, 2015).

3. Marcial Losada and Emily Heaphy, "The Role of Positivity and Connectivity in the Performance of Business Teams: A Nonlinear Dynamics Model," *American Behavioral Scientist* 47, no. 6 (February 2004): 740–65.

4. "The Power and Vestigiality of Positive Emotion—What's Your Happiness Ratio?," Happier Human, 2014, http://happierhuman.com/positivity-ratio/.

5. "Probability of Competing beyond High School," NCAA, 2015, http://www.ncaa.org/about/resources/research/probability-competing-beyond-high-school.

## Chapter 5 I Choose to Let Go of Old Baggage

1. Robert Frost, "The Road Not Taken" (1916), public domain.

2. Terry Hargrave and Franz Pfitzer, *Restoration Therapy: Understanding and Guiding Healing in Marriage and Family Therapy* (New York: Routledge, 2011).

3. William Fleeman, *Managing Anger and Rage: The Niagara Falls Metaphor Video* (Manassas Park, VA: Impact Publications, 2002).

4. Ron Welch, *The Controlling Husband: What Every Woman Needs to Know* (Grand Rapids: Revell, 2014).

## Chapter 6 I Choose to Forgive: Part 1

1. Everett Worthington and Nathaniel Wade, "The Psychology of Unforgiveness and Forgiveness and Implications for Clinical Practice," *Journal of Social and Clinical Psychology* 18, no. 4 (December 1999): 385.

2. Concordia University, "Can Blaming Others Make People Sick?," *Science Daily*, August 11, 2011, https://www.sciencedaily.com/releases/2011/08/110809104259.htm.

3. Michael Linden and Andreas Maercker, *Embitterment: Societal, Psychological, and Clinical Perspectives* (New York: Springer, 2011).

4. Everett Worthington, *The Path to REACH Forgiveness: Less Than Two Hours to Becoming a More Forgiving Person, Self-Directed Learning Workbook* (Richmond, VA: Virginia Commonwealth University, 2011), 9–11.

## Chapter 7 I Choose to Forgive: Part 2

1. David Snarch, "Love and Marriage: Searching for More Passion in the Bedroom," *Today Show*, July 14, 2006.

## Chapter 8 I Choose to Be Unselfish: Part 1

1. Legacy Staff, "The Words of John Wooden: 100 Years of Inspiration," Legacy.com, October 2010, http://www.legacy.com/news/explore-history/article/the-words-of-john-wooden-100-years-of-inspiration.

2. Scott Stanley et al., "Sacrifice as a Predictor of Marital Outcomes," *Family Process* 45, no. 3 (September 2006): 289–303.

3. "Henry David Thoreau Quotes," Got to Know, accessed June 25, 2018, https://www.gotknowhow.com/quotes/henry-david-thoreau-sacrificing-your-happiness-for-the-happiness-of-the-one.

4. Dominik Schoebi, Benjamin Karney, and Thomas Bradbury, "Stability and Change in the First 10 Years of Marriage: Does Commitment Confer Benefits beyond the Effects of Satisfaction?" *Journal of Personality and Social Psychology* 102, no. 4 (April 2012): 729–42.

5. Howard Markman and Scott Stanley, "Assessing Commitment in Personal Relationships," *Journal of Marriage and Family* 54, no. 3 (August 1992): 595–608.

## Chapter 9 I Choose to Be Unselfish: Part 2

1. Gary Chapman, *Now You're Speaking My Language* (Nashville: B&H, 2014), chap. 4, Kindle.

2. Chapman, *Now You're Speaking My Language,* chap. 5, Kindle.

3. Tara Parker-Pope, "The Happy Marriage Is the 'Me' Marriage," *New York Times*, December 31, 2010, WK4.

4. Elizabeth Thomas, *Before You Walk Down the Aisle: A Woman's Guide to Selecting a Lifelong Partner* (Nashville: West Bow Press, 2011), 49.

5. Tim Downs and Joy Downs, *The Seven Conflicts: Resolving the Most Common Disagreements in Marriage* (Chicago: Moody, 2003), chap. 7, Kindle.

6. Tim Keller, *The Meaning of Marriage: Facing the Complexities of Commitment with the Wisdom of God* (New York: Dutton, 2011), 56.

7. Craig Blomberg and Elizabeth Sbanotto, *Effective Generational Ministry: Biblical and Practical Insights for Transforming Church Communities* (Grand Rapids: Baker Academic, 2016), 167–99.

## Chapter 10  I Choose to Challenge "Unspoken Truths"

1. Henry Cloud and John Townsend, *Boundaries: When to Say Yes, How to Say No to Take Control of Your Life* (New York: HarperCollins/ Zondervan, 1992).

## Chapter 11  I Choose to Be Intimate

1. *Merriam-Webster's Collegiate Dictionary*, s.v. "intimacy."

2. *Merriam-Webster's Collegiate Dictionary*, s.v. "intimate."

3. *Merriam-Webster's Collegiate Dictionary*, s.v. "intimate."

4. *Merriam-Webster's Collegiate Dictionary*, s.v. "intimate."

5. Paul Rosenblatt and Elizabeth Wieling, *Knowing and Not Knowing in Intimate Relationships* (New York: Cambridge University Press, 2013).

## Chapter 12  I Choose Not to Take You for Granted

1. John Gottman and Nan Silver, *The Seven Principles for Making Marriage Work* (Danvers, MA: Harmony, 2000), 32–39.

## Chapter 14  I Choose to Trust

1. Ngina Otiende, "Twitter Quotes on Marriage," Marriage Missions International, accessed June 25, 2018, https://marriagemissions.com/twitter-quotes-marriage-page-9/.

2. Martin Seligman, Steven Maier, and James Geer, "Alleviation of Learned Helplessness in the Dog," *Journal of Abnormal Psychology* 73, no. 3 (June 1968): 256–62.

3. *Merriam-Webster's Collegiate Dictionary*, s.v. "integrity."

4. "John Wooden Quotes," Good Reads, 2018, https://www.goodreads.com/author/quotes/23041.John_Wooden.

5. Cheryl Sanders, "Lawrence Kohlberg's Stages of Moral Development," Encyclopedia Brittanica, accessed June 25, 2018, https://www.britannica.com/science/Lawrence-Kohlbergs-stages-of-moral-development.

**Dr. Ron Welch** joined the faculty of Denver Seminary in 2008 and currently serves as professor of counseling. He earned his PsyD and MA from Central Michigan University. He has worked in the field of clinical psychology for over twenty-five years, and he has been a licensed clinical psychologist since 1997.

Dr. Welch began his postdoctoral career in the Federal Bureau of Prisons, where he worked for seven years as a clinical psychologist. He has taught at Crichton College and Colorado Christian University in the psychology department, also serving as the chair of the psychology department at CCU. Since 2004, Dr. Welch has maintained a counseling practice in clinical psychology. He opened his current private practice, Transformational Marriage, PLLC (transformational -marriage.com), in 2011 and focuses on premarital, marital, and family therapy as well as men's issues.

Dr. Welch is the author of the book *The Controlling Husband* (Revell, 2014). He has also authored several articles and book chapters and has presented numerous papers at professional conferences. His research and writing focus on control and power in marital relationships, attachment in adult friendships and marriage, and the relationship between hope and attachment to God.

Dr. Welch has been married to his wife, Jan, for over thirty years. Jan is a Colorado licensed teacher who specializes in working with students with educational challenges. She owned her own nutritional counseling business for many years as well. The couple has two sons, Britton and Brevin, and one grandson.

Website: transformational-marriage.com
Email: help@transformational-marriage.com

# ALSO AVAILABLE
## FROM DR. RON WELCH

In this candid book, Dr. Ron Welch shows how husbands develop controlling behavior and why women sometimes allow themselves to be controlled. He then gives practical strategies to help both husband and wife transform the power and control issues in their marriage.

# TRANSFORMATIONAL
## MARRIAGE COUNSELING
## & SEMINARS

**WWW.TRANSFORMATIONAL-MARRIAGE.COM**

---

- Marriage counseling
- Premarital counseling
- Marriage seminars

---